JULIET

From Slavery to Inspiration

By
Jesse L. Russell

Dedicated To The

Phillips Family

"Lest we Forget"

Jene L. Purnell

A Special Thanks to the following persons:

Laurine Frakes Kennedy
Olga Rojer
Perri Morgan
Dorothy Davis
William Gee
Jane Ailes
Raymond Crafton

Foreword

In the early 1980s I began a search for my roots and during this journey, I uncovered the roots of another family that had become intertwined with my own family in ways I had never suspected. As I dug deeper, a story of human tragedy, hope, love and a persistence to overcome all odds began to unfold. What I had discovered, touched me deeply as well as inspired me. I had no intentions of writing a book about the events and the people involved. It began with writing down the account of my findings and without conscious thought, a story began to develop in far greater detail than I thought possible of myself. The result is a creative non fiction with more fact than fiction.

The characters and events of this story are true, although I have taken the liberty to bring these long ago characters and events to life. In my Author's Notes, I attempt to give specifics regarding truth and fiction. Only two characters are completely fictional and only two events are totally fictional. Both characters and events are only a small part of this story but they should not be taken as inconceivable, for such characters surely existed elsewhere during the time frame of this story.

The primary intent of this book is to hopefully inspire the reader, regardless of race or sex. The secondary intent is to provide some light on a small but important part of the history of our country. Although moral lessons can certainly be taken from this story, it was not written for that express purpose. If the reader takes nothing more from this story than an inspiration to their own lives, then I have achieved my main goal.

Even though I know less about the main character, Juliet, than many of others in this story, I found her to be an inspiration to me personally. It was Juliet who was the key figure in her family and the key figure in her quest for freedom in an 8 year long, grueling court battle. If I could go back in time, Juliet would be one of the first persons I would seek out. So many questions swirling around Juliet still abound, but fortunately, I have been able to trace a part of her family to present times and through them I have been afforded a distant glimpse of Juliet.

Juliet, her daughter Harriet and their descendants have been an inspiration to the author. Knowledge of our past and knowledge in all it's forms, is what conveys us from the darkness of ignorance and delivers us to enlightenment.

May each of you who reads this story become enlightened…...*and inspired.*

Chapter 1
The University of Pittsburgh School of Pharmacy
The Year 1916

Ella Phillips stood proudly in front of her small wall mirror that had become slightly clouded with age adjusting her graduation cap. Once she was satisfied with the positioning of her cap she continued to stare into the mirror as the reflection of her face faded into a reflection of her life. Although unbeknownst to her, her journey had been centuries in the making, but for now her thoughts only reached back to the memories of her own life that had molded her into the proud and strong woman she had become.

Much of Ella's childhood had been spent with her grandparents. One a former slave and the other, a former slave owner. Together, they had encouraged her to come live with them in town where she could be near a school for black children. Typical of all schools then, whether it be for whites or for blacks, it was nothing more than a small one room structure of dubious construction that seemed to invite little more than a stiff breeze that would relegate it to debatable history as to where it may have once stood. Within it's poorly built walls were children of all ages and degrees of educational proficiency.....and she loved every moment of it.

Her grandmother, Harriet, had been determined that each of her children took full advantage of school, such as it was, and she demanded the same of her grandchildren. Harriet instinctively knew that education was the only way that the old chains of bondage could be cast aside once and forever.

On this day of graduation, Ella could feel the presence of her grandmother. Ella had achieved what many had thought was nothing more than the fanciful dreams of a child. Although her grandmother had grown up as a slave and was denied what was now a basic right to education, she had more than made up for her lack of formal education with a wisdom that cannot be taught in a school, but rather learned over decades of a willingness to observe the subtle and sometimes not so subtle lessons that life provided. When Ella had first recognized her grandmother's wisdom was the first day of her own path to wisdom. Today, Ella realized that one's education cannot survive without the wisdom to implement it. They stand like two columns supporting the same structure.

Ella was older than most of her classmates. She had left for the all black Storer College in nearby Harpers Ferry when she was only 12 years old and graduated at age 16. But, as life would have it, she fell in love, married and had a child. These were memories that would torment her for the rest of her life. Her child died three years later of illness and her marriage began to fall apart shortly thereafter. Certainly God must have had a plan, but the cruelness of His plan was nearly too much for her to bear. A deep and debilitating depression left her floundering in currents that pulled her further and further away from the safety of shore. Although the loss of her child and the subsequent dissolution of her marriage had opened another door to her life, she would have sacrificed all that she now achieved for the life of her child. How many times had she heard that God worked in mysterious ways? These simple words never gave the comfort they were meant to give, but she had in time accepted the dueling fate of her life, but to say she felt comfort would have to be left to others who had been blessed not to have walked in her shoes. With her degree in pharmacy nearly in hand, maybe her knowledge of medicine could save a yet unknown child thus cheating death of it's indiscriminate feeding on the young and sparing a young mother from the torturous loss of their own child.

   Today's events stirred a cauldron of emotions for Ella. Her inner strength had always been her shield and sword. Today it would be no different, nor would it differ throughout her life. Strength of mind and soul was no stranger to her family and like a family heirloom, this strength was passed on from generation to generation from mother to daughter, beginning with a woman named Juliet.

   Juliet's name would never perish in hearts and minds of her family. Many years before, in those dark days of slavery, Juliet's inner strength had inspired her children and her children's children to fight to the end and then more. Ella knew that if her great grandmother had endured all that slavery had thrown at her, that she should certainly be able to survive whatever life, even in it's most vile moments, could throw at her. It was Juliet's words, passed down to Harriet and then down to her, that Ella now thought: *"If you don't jump in the pond, then you ain't nevuh gonna swim"*.

   Those simple words had unconsciously put a small smile on her face when a single, short knock on the door brought her back to the present. Without being asked to come in, a man's head appeared around the side of the door. Ella seemed to recognize the smile on his face before she recognized the face. It seemed odd to her that a person's face could be so secondary to a mere smile, yet it seemed natural at the same time. Maybe the smile and what it represented to her was the nature of love's effect on the mind. Seeing his smile was like panacea to all her past sadness. It never ceased to lift her spirits, not to mention that it also sent a small shiver of excitement through her. He had been the only other black classmate in the School of Pharmacy, but more than that, he had been her best friend, lover and now, future husband. Miss Ella Nora Phillips would soon become Mrs William Wyatt Stewart.

Bill quietly said, "Are you ready, Ella?"

Ella replied, "Maybe the better question would be, 'Is the world ready for me!'"

"I fear that the world is getting you whether it likes it or not", replied Bill.

Laughing, Ella rejoindered, "Maybe the world won't like it, but the world is my cherry and it will not be taken away from me! And if they try, they will get nothing but the pit and it will be their loss, not mine."

Bill chuckled and said, "And that would not be a world I would wish to live in!

Bill then returned to his immediate duty and said, "If we don't get a move on, we'll miss our own graduation and that cherry of yours is going to taste just a wee bit sour." Bill said while throwing his arms around her.

"Careful there big boy! You're going to mess up a good hour of trying to get this cap just right on my head!" Ella jokingly said.

Bill released his arms from around her and then offered his arm in an exaggerated gentlemanly fashion where Ella took it and said, "Here we come world! Like it or not!"

Chapter 2
Juliet's World Upside Down
Court 1848

The shouting and taunts had begun.

"Nigger!" yelled one man.

"Born a slave and you gonna die a slave" shouted another.

Juliet, who was normally a strong willed woman, was now frightened. Her eyes darted from one shout to the next. Her eyes widened with both alertness and fear. As late as yesterday, she had looked forward to her day in court. Now, she wondered whether her pursuit of her dream would end before she even entered the white man's court.

The shouting mob of local townsfolk began to merge into an indistinct roar, leaving Juliet light headed and nauseous. Her faintness was suddenly interrupted by an object that struck her head. Although the rock had only grazed her, she nevertheless felt a sharp sting, followed by the warmth of her own blood trickling beneath the red scarf tied around her head. Rather than being dazed by her minor head injury, it seemed to have awakened her from her fear induced drift into the safe world of unconsciousness.

She could not understand how freedom could be considered anything other than a God given right and was confused as to how it had gotten to the point of white men making the decision as to who was free and who was not. But, she had no question as to her right to fight for that which was an inalienable right for *every* living soul on this earth. As she had always said, *If you don't jump in the pond, you nevuh gonna swim.*

   Most of the men who insulted and threatened her were lowly
and mean. Little more than slaves themselves except for their
color. They were part of a societal pecking order where their
seemingly only goal was not so much as to move up the ladder,
but to keep themselves from sinking any lower. And this type
man who gathered here today was intent upon not falling to the
lowest rung of the ladder as a result of a favorable verdict to
Juliet. Without slavery, this lowly group of men would find
themselves equals and they had no intention of being an equal to a
Negro.

   Juliet turned to the attorney who represented her today and
bluntly asked, "Why do you stand beside me today and argue for
my freedom?"

   Her attorney paused before answering and realized that he had
not yet come to a clear reason as why he decided to represent her.
He was of average height but his deep set dark eyes and strong
face made him appear taller than he actually was. Surprisingly,
his voice was soft and Juliet wondered whether he would be able
to be heard, let alone have the legal skills necessary to obtain the
freedom she had once been promised nearly a decade before.

   Parker came from an old and distinguished Virginia family.
His grandfather had been a colonel in the War for Independence
and after the war become a successful attorney that helped him
purchase large tracts of land. On one of these tracts snuggled in
between the Blue Ridge and Shenandoah River, he built his
magnificent home. His father had followed in his grandfather's
footsteps and he had followed in his father's footsteps. Parker
still lived in the stately home that his grandfather had built, who
named it "Soldier's Retreat" that most people called just "The

Retreat."   The Parker family had become wealthy and in no small part from the labor of their slaves. The degree of a man's wealth

in Virginia was more times than not, proportionately related to the number of slaves he owned and the Parker's were correspondingly wealthy.

Parker thought before answering Juliet. It would have been easy to just tell Juliet that it was an attorney's job to separate themselves from any personal feelings and to allow the law to be his guide. But, he knew that this case was far more than just the law. This case was about human bondage and the immorality of an institution that treated men, women and children as little more than chattle. He was not an abolitionist by any stretch of the imagination, but as an attorney, it was his nature to question laws and to answer them within the parameters of the US Constitution and the Bill of Rights. There had never been a written document that could compare to the rights this living piece of political and philosophical art provided to a nation's people, but in reality, the continuation of slavery also made the Constitution one of the most hypocritical documents ever written. If it was "self evident" that all men were created equal, then the evidence was sorely lacking as long as slavery existed. The debates that resulted in the constitution were often heated and old friendships had been left bloodied on the floor of those early Continental Congress'. Slavery had, among many other issues, been one of those strongly debated items, but in the end, that issue too had been left trampled and bloodied on those same sacred floors of independence. Now, 65 years since the country had secured their independence, the question of slavery could no longer be brushed aside and left to gather dust. A movement to end slavery had been growing steadily in the northern states and was now gathering a head of steam with each passing year. Parker knew that in one way or the other, a day of reckoning would come and that more than likely, it would be sooner than later.

   After an extended pause before answering Juliet's question, Parker settled for the lawyerly reply, "I wrote that will for Mr. Crafton and believe that his true intentions were to free you and the others from bondage and I feel that I must defend his last will and testament as I know it to be."

   This was true, but it was not completely honest with Juliet, or with himself. The abolition movement had moved from the fringes to center stage. Northern congressmen were now openly supporting the movement and the shock waves were rippling throughout not only the old northern states, but now to those territories recently admitted to the Union and likewise to those territories that were seeking admittance to the Union. The anti-slavery voice was impatient and ceaseless. He knew that the agrarian South, who relied on slavery to build personal wealth, would not stand idly by but would do what they felt necessary to protect their way of life. The question was, would the end of slavery come as a result of cooler heads prevailing or would it end in blood? Wars had been fought in the name of many things, but when it's thin veneer of pseudo-morality was removed, all wars, at their core, are fought to defend one's power and wealth. Parker hoped he was wrong about the possibility of war, but history would suggest otherwise. It had only been a generation ago that his own family had fought for their country's independence and with the American victory, a Union was formed. Now, that same Union was beginning to show the symptoms of an old wound that had never been treated and was beginning to fester….and that wound was called slavery.

   As Parker reached the court house door he heard someone shout, "Traitor!" He knew that word was meant for him. His life had been the law and he felt comfortable within the confines of law but the emotional outburst he was witnessing today sent a perceptible shiver through him. Emotion had always been the

enemy of rational thought, and the tightly coiled emotions in these unruly mob of men reigned supreme within their limited intellect.

Rock Hall Farm
facing west towards Winchester, Virginia

Chapter 3
The Old Man

Nature provides it's own unique form of music. It can be as soft and fleeting as a blush, and at other times harsh and unforgiving. Our own lives dance to these same rhythms and changes in tempo. Tonight the old man found himself drifting in and out of thought to the chorus of hundreds of young peepers signaling the end of winter. Aging brings an acuteness of appreciation of little things that youth inadvertently dulls with it's quest for larger things. Tonight a mixture of joy and sadness began to weave it's way through the old man like two single fibers spinning on a loom. Little by little these strands create the whole. Woven intrinsically together.

Several months earlier he had been inflicted with a partial paralysis to one side of his body. He had suffered a stroke which was an insult to injury. He had been left stooped through years by the simple act of sitting on a buckboard and then having his spine assaulted by bone rattling journeys on roads rutted beyond recognition. He had seen the malady of paralysis in others and knew that the end could either be swift, or unmercifully imprison it's victim for years. But, what was certain, was that death had given notice.

There was much to do before he was taken from this earth. As he looked out his window his eyes involuntarily led him to the site of the old family graveyard on a hill some 800 feet away. He thought of those who went before him, lowering them into the stubborn reddish clay soils that were prominent in this part of the county. Always they were laid to rest with their head facing west and their feet facing east. In this manner, one's soul would would rise from the grave facing the sunrise. The death and then rebirth of the day assisting the rebirth of the soul. The alpha and the omega. He accepted this old tradition but now he thought that a man's true rebirth should begin while he still lived and not rely on death to wipe away one's sins in order to be reborn. The thought of an eternal life provided for him little comfort. If eternal life brought such joy, then should we not throw ourselves upon our swords in order to quicken our journey to the great, *joyful,* eternity? And furthermore, God *knows!* that if he had one more Baptist preacher trying to save his soul that he might be driven to help *them* on their way to their own precious desire for eternal life!

Damned preachers were like locust invading every street corner, and any other strategic place where they could trap supposed sinners, he silently mused. To the mind of the predatory preacher, there were no shortage of sinners. Possibly these preachers were right, but he had seen enough preachers to know that they more often than not, spoke out of both sides of their mouth. He had on occasion mentioned to others of like mind that if it weren't for sinners, preachers might actually have to *work* for a living.

To be on the safe side, he quickly asked forgiveness for calling a preacher, *damned.* He ended his thoughts on religion for now, as he had more important things to think about.

The old man's name was John Russell Crafton, but for the most part, other than for the most important of legal documents, he had gone by the abridged and more economical name of Russell, the maiden name of his mother. He had only been 4 years old when his father left in 1776 to join the 6th NC Militia at the onset of war with England. What little he knew of his father had come from his mother. His father had been involved with the import/export business, and dabbled in both the law and surveying. Old John Russell (Crafton) figured that North Carolina must have liked "dabblers" because he had been made an Adjutant to a NC Militia with the rank of Major. He never returned to Virginia to be with his family, but remained in South Carolina when the war had shifted from the northern colonies to the southern colonies. He had remained in the army until the bitter end and died in SC less than 2 years after the Treaty of Paris was signed between England and America in 1783. His father, Bennett Crafton, left his entire estate to an elder son. Not unusual for the eldest son to inherit everything, and for the other sons left to fend for themselves. He did not hold any grudge against the father he barely remembered. Without money, his mother had indentured him to an old friend of his father's who was also in the import/export business, when he was only 12 years old. Goods needed to be transported and his father's old friend had put him with one of his teamsters. Within 8 years he had started his own teamster business, owning several wagons and a number of horses. It had not made him rich by any means, but it did provide a reasonable living.

John Russell (Crafton) had named his eldest son Bennett, after his own father, as was the custom of the times. He had made sure that all his children could read, write and do their numbers, but it was his son Bennett who had apparently inherited Major Bennett Crafton's sharp mind…..as well as his ambition. With little or nothing to help get him started in life, he had purchased 245 acres in the northern Shenandoah Valley which in time would grow to more than 1,900 acres before he died in 1862. Young Bennett would capitalize on the poor weather conditions that ravaged England and Europe for years which resulted in a wheat shortage which in turn drove the price of wheat skyward. So, Bennett grew wheat and sold it for record high prices, which he then parlayed into more and more properties adjacent to his original tract of land. Wheat had made him, if not wealthy, certainly on the cusp of wealth.

As both his wealth and family grew, he enlarged the old log home with a stone L shaped wing and then covered the entire dwelling with an exterior plaster- like material that shrouded it's humble beginnings. Like many of the homes at this time, they were one room deep with fireplaces in the center of the house so that one fireplace could heat at least 2 rooms comfortably. A columned porch ran across the length of the house. A doorway on the second floor led out to the flat roof over the porch. Second story porches were not so much an architectural feature as much as it was to provide the residents relief from the insects in the summer (most insects as a rule only fly approximately 6 feet off the ground and the upper porch clearly exceeded 6 feet). Even though the upper porch was only 10 feet above grade, it was enough to capture small breezes that were not commonly felt at ground level. It was at this home of Bennett's that his father, John Russell, now resided in his fading years.

Bennett Russell's (he too went by the Russell name now) farm, known as Rock Hall, was situated in a lush, narrow valley with views of the Blue Ridge to the east and the Allegheny's to the west. The home sat at the intersection of two main roads. One was the Alexandria road that connected both Alexandria and Winchester and the other connected to Jefferson County where the confluence of the Shenandoah and Potomac rivers occurred. Bennett was not one to miss an opportunity and his home was located perfectly to take advantage of the travelers who needed a meal and a room for the night before continuing their travels the next day. At the intersection of these two main roads, he built a small general store to further take advantage of the ever increasing numbers of travelers, and unlike those early immigrants to this area approximately 100 years ago, these travelers had money in their pockets......which Bennett was more than willing to help lighten their *financial burden.*

Rock Hall
Home of Bennett Russell

Photo taken circa 1858
Bennett Russell shown center left with white beard

Like every other day in his life, the old man woke before sunrise. His partial paralysis had to some extent improved, but he found it still difficult to do the little things he had always taken for granted. Getting out of bed by himself had become a chore and the lighting of the old lantern on the small walnut table by his bed was an effort to keep from accidentally burning the house down as he shakily fumbled to put the match to the wick and then place the throat of the glass hurricane between the four prongs holding the glass in place. He felt like a small child carelessly fumbling with the simplest of tasks. Dressing himself resulted in buttons left open or at best, buttons placed through the wrong holes, leaving him looking more bent and twisted than he actually was. The energy he used to just get dressed always left him exhausted and frustrated. With his dexterity compromised, he had asked Juliet to place his clothes on the dresser instead of in the dresser.

Juliet had always been a large part of his life, from hitching up the horses to the wagon, loading and unloading goods to be transported, cooking meals, feeding the horses, cleaning tack and a hundred other small tasks, but now she had become indispensable in an entirely different way. She had also been indispensable to his own family. Juliet, even though a slave, had in many ways taken over the role of a mother to his own children. The old man's wife had died when most of the children still needed a mother. Juliet filled the role of mother to his younger children and it was apparent that she did so not just out of a slave's obligation to her master, but with a heartfelt affection towards the children. Children were children, regardless of color. Juliet knew that some day, a child's innocent color blindness would eventually devolve into a stark contrast of black and white, with morality, as it has always been, an ever changing shade of gray.

It was hard to pinpoint where Juliet got her strength and her pride. Like most people, we are the product of both nature and nurture. Being a slave, nurture would in all likelihood, not play a large role. Slaves are taught at a young age to respect their masters and even fear them, so nurture and nature were often at odds with one another. One thing is certain, pride and strength does not come to a slave through the nurturing of their masters. Although, like any child, they learn through observation. Possibly, Juliet had watched and then mimicked one of her own parents before being taken from them to be sold to the *old man*. But, watching and learning often take a lifetime to become what we become. It would be more likely, that Juliet was born with these traits and yes, possibly reinforced by observing her parents own characteristics, but the old man was a firm believer in that God makes the major decisions, barring any interference from *preachers*. In His hands we are just so much clay, to be molded as He sees fit.

People who were under the conventional impression that slaves were nothing more than children who were incapable of learning little more than basic chores and farm work, were only deceiving themselves, but if they did truly believe the slave was intellectually limited and never be able to read and write, then why were there laws against a slave learning to read and write? The South was full of contradictions.......especially when it came to slavery.

Juliet had listened when the old man was counting items in his wagon and had quietly and surreptitiously learned her numbers through observation. She had done the same with learning some of her letters by seeing a label on some item and then hearing the name of it said out loud. It wasn't the art of reading so much as a system of selective reading. No one had taught her the alphabet, and this left her at a serious disadvantage, although her unique system did bear some fruit. Once when the old man, without thinking, asked her to get 12 bags of corn meal off the wagon, Juliet did just that. It suddenly dawned on old man Crafton later that day that somewhere along the line, Juliet had incredibly learned the basic concept of numbers and even maybe letters. He was suspicious of someone having taught her behind his back, but he realized: first, that there would never have been time for anyone to teach her and secondly, most of the men that they had been around in her life were illiterate and couldn't even count the fingers on their hands. The thought that she had learned this on her own by just watching and listening, shocked him at first and went against everything he had been told about slaves. This revelation left him stunned at first, then with a realization that should have always been apparent, that Negroes were as human and as intelligent as any other person, regardless of color. On this day the old man had an epiphany that was more comparable to the ludicrous discovery that a fish could swim. Nevertheless, his world had been shaken and some things for him would never be the same.

She deserved much better, and today, he would take the first step in putting his plan in motion.

Chapter 4
Reflections

As the old man sat in the split bottom chair in his sparsely furnished bedroom, his memories flooded back to a time when he was young and to the time when he first saw his wife to be. She had come to this country when she was 10 years old from Scotland. All said, she was not what one would call a classically beautiful woman, but she made up for that with both a remarkable spirit and startling green eyes. He had never quite seen green eyes like hers and struggled to make a proper comparison, but it was her spirit at an open air market that had first got his attention.

She had been berating an itinerant merchant with her nearly unintelligible Scottish brogue for attempting to cheat her. Berating may be an understatement. She had grabbed the man by his long unkempt hair and slammed his head down to the top of the merchant's table. John Russell Crafton was 26 years old when he first laid eyes on her and like everyone else at the market he turned to see what the commotion was all about. The unsavory man's cheating, followed by his rude and curse filled denial, had ignited her Scottish ire to it's fullest extent. In his travels, he had met many Scotsmen and knew that these oddly speaking people were quick to anger, but on the other hand were hard working, independent, loyal and embraced life with an odd mixture of humor and accepted tribulation of life. Had the argument only been an angry exchange of words, John Russell Crafton would have seen nothing outside the ordinary and would have never met his future wife. But it had escalated beyond words and fate waited with open arms.

Suddenly the odoriferous merchant broke free of her grip on his disheveled begrimed hair and without compunction, knocked her to the ground with a loose board from the top of his makeshift table. As he raised the board to strike her again, John grabbed the man's arm. It was apparent that the merchant was no stranger to quarreling and his face showed the scars and facial bone breaks that disfigured an already unpleasant countenance. But Crafton, being a teamster, he had to be able to pit his own strength against the strength of his horses….. or find another line of work. And as a result of this nearly daily activity, it had created in John noticeably strong shoulders, back and arms. The vile and foul merchant had taken notice of John's physique, but also of as his eyes that had threateningly transformed from their normal bright blue to a bluish coal like color. If the merchant had learned anything over his many years, it was an ability to not only size up a man's physical attributes, but to be able to read a man and quickly determine if they could be bluffed or not. The grimy and half toothless merchant took no time in making the decision that retreat was the better part of valor. Honor was for the fools who either intentionally or not, courted death. He may not have had an ounce of honor but he was no fool either, when it came to primal decisions.

John then reached down to help this small, feisty lass back to her feet. She was still wary and paused for a moment before taking John's hand. In that brief pause, their eyes met and for John, those green eyes, still fiery with residual anger, changed his life forever.

They were married within months of first meeting and John's memories of her brought a small smile to his face that morning as he prepared for the day. What most folks would have thought strange, if they knew, Juliet reminded John of his now departed wife, Ann. The lithe and feisty lass from Scotland. Not of course in appearance, as she was black with coal black eyes, but comparatively in the same spirit his late wife had. Confident, intelligent and even though a slave, strong and not to be crossed. Some of the local folks felt that Juliet didn't give him the deference that a slave should give her master, but they didn't really know her as he knew her. Most thought of black people as something not quite human. Indeed they were treated the same as chattel that could be bought and sold at the whim of their owners. He had once been one of these people, but in the fading light of his life, he saw more than black faces, but saw instead people of flesh and blood, who cried, who laughed, who were not so much unlike himself other than color and their plight in life. Time had changed all of that and a slow rolling moral manifestation worked it's way into his consciousness much like hearing far off sounds in your sleep only to suddenly awake and realize that the sounds he had subconsciously heard were in fact real.

As a younger man he was like most others in Virginia, seldom giving much thought to slavery. It was what it was. No more. No less. Why he had come to seriously considering the morality of slavery had in some ways come as a surprise to him. He was aware that with age came the inevitable reflection on one's life. Had he been a bit more cognizant of this fact, he might not have been surprised that his changing view on slavery would have held a more prominent place during his reflective moments.

As we near the end of our time on earth, it is natural to reflect on one's own life. That which we have done well and that which we question. The latter can manifest itself with a desire to atone for misdeeds, or to mend fences with those who had become distant for reasons long forgotten and stubbornly continued. Youth too often suppresses humility and courts folly. Wisdom is the byproduct of our own mistakes and misjudgments. It more often than not slumbers within us and only awakens when we accept impending mortality. The old man welcomed this awakening and was suddenly flooded with emotion. Tears, mixed with both joy and sadness, coursed down his weathered face and fell silently on the childishly unaligned buttons of his shirt. Old age revolts against the simplest of physical tasks and at the same time exerts an acuteness of compassion. This trade off seemed to him so unfair, but he knew that this was the mystery of life that takes on one hand and provides on the other hand. The fading light illuminates one's chance to correct our wrongs. It is the bathing within this fading light that for some, are given a chance to cleanse a part of our soul. John Russell Crafton had accepted his baptism, not of meaningless water, but something far exceeding the ritual of a church.

Chapter 5
Hope

John left the bedroom and scattered rays of sun light now softly flowed on the floors and walls. These disjointed streams of alternating degrees of visibility would slowly unify into the benevolent light of day. He noticed how the newly born rays of sunshine would always expose the tiny particles of dust that floated softly through the air, only to seemingly disappear in their hidden flight within the fabric of the sun's growing intensity. During the still of the night, the dust, seeming to have tired of their aimless flight, would wearily come to roost upon their man made nests until once again awoken by the intrusion of the sun's early rays of light.

He stood momentarily at a window looking west at a patch of low marshland on the farm which was fed by intermittent springs that seeped only when the ground had been saturated by rainfall. The marsh would attract the Great Blue Herons and white egrets and the sight of these long legged birds feeding from the richness of the marsh reminded him of his childhood home in the marshy lands of tidewater Virginia. This western view took him to his distant past. The eastern view from the opposite window, that overlooked the graveyard took him unsettling close to his future.

The old man shook away his memories.....as well as his thoughts on death, and walked over to his secretary. The desk was a source of pride for him. He had purchased it on a trip to Baltimore in 1800. The secretary had 4 drawers and a solid roll top inlaid with a large oval of a darker type of wood. With the top lifted up into a matching angled slot and out of sight, a hidden desk top could then be slid forward creating a flat working area.

With the working part of the desk exposed, 3 small drawers were located on either side, with a larger locked compartment as it's centerpiece that was adorned with an inlaid eagle holding arrows in the talons of both feet. In actuality, Bennett, the eldest son of Crafton had furnished most of the house with both utilitarian and quality furniture. The sideboard was Hepplewhite and the dining room table and the 8 chairs around it had been made by one of the top furniture makers in the Valley. Additional chairs and tables were solidly constructed but in a more primitive design. But, the exquisite secretary was his. A fine piece of craftsmanship for an old teamster to own, he thought to himself.

The rest of the family shortly followed and gathered at the table for breakfast. Breakfast consisted of boiled oats and hard bread during the work week. Sunday breakfast was more elaborate, consisting of eggs, grits, cured ham and fried potatoes seasoned with onions and bacon fat. When his son Bennett finished breakfast, it was a signal for his own sons that breakfast was over and work was to begin. Once Bennett and the boys had left for their daily duties, John Russell Crafton decided that it was time to have a talk with Juliet.

The old man awkwardly struggled to slide his chair back from the secretary, but once accomplished, called out, "Juliet. Could I see you for a moment?"

Juliet walked towards the room the old man used as his office, wiping her hands on her apron. The apron had been patched so many times it resembled a small version of the patchwork quilt on his bed. On her head was her ubiquitous red scarf. It had once been a bright red, but was now faded to a dull pink. Although her complexion was as black as black could be, her features were more like a white persons. Thin and sharp. She always drew curious stares when she accompanied the old man to town to get supplies. Most white men had the odd notion that her features were the exclusive domain of the white man and that she had somehow infringed upon their right of appearance. At the same time these same men were intrigued with her beauty and found that to be unsettling. They also resented that she made them feel this way.

White Women, while in the presence of Juliet, was another story all together! Old Mrs. Cobb had once said in a show of exaggerated offense "How dare she!" No explanation had been needed. The other old hens with her knew exactly what she had meant. What Mrs. Cobb and her women friends didn't know, or refused to face, was that their reaction to Juliet stemmed mostly from jealousy.

When Juliet entered the room she replied to the old man's instructions, "What be on your mind, Mr. John?"

Crafton replied, "Today, the lawyer, Mr. Parker is coming to visit. Do you know why he is coming by?"

"If'n I knew Mr. John, then there hardly be no reason for me to have walked all the way in here, would it then?"

Most would have considered Juliet's reply as having been impertinent and they would not have been far wrong, but this was Juliet's way, normally infuriating when your patience was already worn thin by other matters, but the old man had long ago gotten use to her manner and merely grunted.

The old man's speech was slow and deliberate as a result of his paralysis but answered, "Mr. Parker is coming by to help me write my Last Will and Testament."

Juliet didn't make any reply but made it clear that she was

listening and was waiting for him to reply to his own question. Her silence did not mean that she wasn't curious as to why he felt any need to share this information with her. So, she quietly waited for the old man to just spit it out.

"Juliet. You and your man Moses, along with your children as well as the others have been with me for some time now. It has been my decision that upon my death that all of you shall be freed."

Juliet momentarily froze, feeling if she had entered a world that was neither here nor there. She wasn't even sure she had heard the old man correctly and feared that if she said anything, this moment would be lost forever, but if her mind was playing tricks on her, it was a cruel trick indeed. She suddenly realized that she hadn't been breathing and took a deep breath.

"Sir?" Juliet said, not trusting her own ears.

"You suddenly gone dumb in the head, girl? I said that when I die, you and the others will be free, but don't go in get any ideas about my death, ya hear?" the old man stated in grim humor.

"So why you tellin' me this now?" questioned Juliet.

Before the old man answered her, he thought this was just like her to be one step ahead of him. Her intelligence was both a blessing and a curse to him at times. This time it seemed to fall somewhere in the middle, so he answered, "I'm telling you this now because upon my death, my boys may not be too terribly happy with my decision."

Juliet replied, "They's got their own slaves. Why would they care?"

The old man frankly replied, "Everybody cares about money….. and you, and the others represent money. Maybe they won't care, but I wanted you to know because once I'm dead and gone, I'll be dead and gone, and won't be able to come back from the grave to argue with them or to pull your arse out of the fire.. One of the blessings of being dead, I suppose."

Juliet could only respond with, "Thank you, suh" and then turned to walk out and added, "bout time suh."

John thought to himself, "damn girl! She just can't for the life of her just be appreciative and accept something for what it is!" Most men don't like women with strength. They called it attitude. They damn sure won't like a freed black woman with "attitude." She was strong willed. That was for sure. With him, he could protect her from harm from others, but when she became free, she would not have him to protect her and so he worried for her future well being.

Juliet thought to herself that she did not wish death on anyone, but if the Lord so chose to take the old man away soon and give her that promised freedom tomorrow, then who was *she* to argue with God.

Chapter 5
Some Snakes Can Walk

That same day Juliet received news of her eventual freedom, she prepared lunch for the Crafton boys –she still thought of them as Craftons on occasion –- and the other slaves in the field. Today, they were all working a good distance from home so she took the old mule and placed the food in sacks that she threw across the neck and shoulders of the beast. She needed to talk to her man Moses and the others but could not tell them anything quite yet. She needed to think first. The news of their future freedom was too good not to share, but she needed to be sure that none of the others would do anything foolish to jeopardize the promise of freedom.

As she neared the group of men she steered clear of Jenkins, the overseer. She had recently overheard some white men in town using a term she had never heard of before. The term was white trash and apparently white men had started using this term to describe other white men, what best that she could understand were lazy, ignorant and in general, mean spirited. White trash was too good of a term for Jenkins. The slaves considered him the spawn of the devil himself. He delighted in the agony and despair of others with a hideous relish. He seldom bathed and his face and neck held an assortment of festering sores and carbuncles. Most people made it a point to stand up wind from him so as to not have his scent attach itself to their own clothing. On the rare occasion when he smiled, he did so only at the pain and misfortune of others. Death would be too kind for this man but she certainly wouldn't argue if death carried his rotting soul away. But so far, even death had rejected his membership to the world beyond.

Juliet's next to youngest child had followed her mother to the fields that day to bring lunch to the workers. Harriet was only 3 years old, but showed an innate sweetness that made her a favorite of not only her mother's, but her older sisters as well. She was light skinned for a child of Juliet's and although she knew Harriet was the daughter of Moses, she assumed that she had inherited the light skin of her grandmother who was considered a mulatto. From Moses, she inherited the kind and compassionate disposition. From her mother, she had inherited the small, sharp features that made Juliet standout among the slave population in general. She had also inherited Juliet's quick mind. For the past 5 weeks Harriet had affectionately carried her kitten around with her with the ever present and inseparable brother Marshall in tow, and today was no exception.

The field work today consisted of clearing rock breaks. While doing so, the men had stumbled across a den of copperheads. It was early spring and the snakes were beginning to feel the warmth of the day and stir from their long winter hibernation. They had become agitated from the abrupt intrusion by man, but were famished from the months of deep sleep. The combination of hunger and the unexpected invasion of their protective den, made the snakes more aggressive than usual for a reptile who by all accounts, was naturally aggressive.

The men jumped back when having discovered this den of nasty serpents and shouted to all within hearing distance what they had found. Copperheads were Jenkins' greatest fear yet at the same time, he could not help himself to gaze upon them as they slowly slithered over and around one another.

Jenkins shuddered at the thought of falling into a den of these dangerous snakes but it did not prevent him from doing an act so abhorrent that all who were there that day had fervently wished and even some prayed, for his death to come in a slow and painful way.

As little Harriet curiously approached the men near the copperhead den, Jenkins suddenly snatched the kitten out of Harriet's arms. A hideous smile came across Jenkins' slowly rotting face, and looked at everyone there while holding the small squirming kitten roughly by the neck.

Before Jenkins through the kitten into the den of copperheads, he merely said, "These here snakes look to be hungry." With that, Jenkins tossed the small cat into the copperhead's lair.

The sound emanating from this innocent creature as it was attacked by the copperheads froze everyone. If an animal could cry like a human, then this was the sickening sound they heard. The kitten squirmed and jerked spasmodically with every fanged attack. The sound brought tears to the eyes of everyone, save Jenkins himself. He stood mesmerized over the den watching the horror than took place below him. He only lost interest when all movement of the kitten had ceased.

Moses swept the sobbing and heartbroken little Harriet up in his arms, holding her tightly, while streams of tears fell from his own face. The rest stared at Jenkins with such hatred that he actually felt some fear for his life and abruptly walked away. Juliet had to control every emotion within her to keep from killing Jenkins. She thought to herself that a time would come and when it did, she would act without hesitation. No matter how long it would take, she would get her revenge.

Chapter 6
Sharing the News

That night, Juliet planned to share the news of their foreseeable freedom. Earlier that evening all but Juliet had all gathered to praise the Lord in songs created by slaves and passed on from one generation to another. Their gospel sings were more than just an exercise in religion. It was also a means to socialize, to find relief from the drudgery of work as a slave, and in some cases, to make plans for escape and to pass on where safe houses were located that would assist in their run for freedom. Juliet had been finishing up chores around the manor house, but now joined the others.

"Keep singing," she whispered with a commanding intensity.

One by one she told them the news and one by one their singing became louder, more joyful and ....more heavenly.

Marshall, headstrong and excitable, whispered loudly, "I want to shout this to the heavens!"

Juliet replied, "You shout this out to anyone, and this goes for *all* of you, I will personally tie your skinny little tails in a knot! Our freedom and our lives may depend on us staying as quiet as those little peepers are loud. Y'all hear me? Now do ya?"

One didn't cross Juliet and each nodded their head in the affirmative. Nothing more needed to be said. She had planted the seed of hope and for now, that was all she wanted to do. Give them hope. In her opinion, hope was the nourishment and salvation of the soul and without it, God's children were lost to walk a barren land somewhere between heaven and earth.

Chapter 7
Roadblock to Freedom

Several years had passed since Juliet had been told of their eventual freedom. During the same period of time, the old man had suffered another stroke, but his body wasn't ready to give up yet. It would take 6 more years before John Russell Crafton died and the road to freedom for Juliet and her family could then begin their journey. Freedom for Juliet and the others were tied to the old man's death and no one could predict when that would occur. The uncertainty of it all only made it more difficult to bear for Juliet. It was like reaching out for the brass ring, but never quite being able to reach it. The years crawled by and the brass ring that was to be their freedom remained tantalizing out of reach.

Indeed, the will did provide for the slaves freedom, but John's oldest son, Bennett, had clandestinely written a second will that was referred to as the Articles of Agreement. In these so called Articles, not only was their freedom revoked, but they were to be sold! The agreement between John Russell Crafton and his children was signed in 1842. It later became apparent to Juliet that the old man's sons had found out about the original will that provided for their freedom, and after the old mans second stroke, John's sons needed to act quickly in order to protect their inheritance. As the old man laid on what everyone thought was his deathbed, Bennett's son, who had found out the contents of the original Will, had hurriedly written up a second will.

Old man Crafton laid in his bed, unable to speak and unable to even lift his hand. The room was dark and had that unmistakable pallor of death about it, but unknown to all of them at the time, death wasn't ready to claim the old man. The air was stale and the old man's face was sallow with age and long term sickness. Three of his sons and one other witness had brought chairs in from the dining room and placed them around his bed in expectancy of death. To Bennett, it was now or never and he now stood and walked to the old man's bedside with a written document in his hand. The document was titled "Articles of Agreement". An ink well and pen had earlier been conveniently laid out on the bedside table. Bennett leaned in close to the old man and whispered in his ear. What was said would never be known. One couldn't speak and the other wouldn't speak. Any funeral arrangements the family may have made were premature, as he lingered for another grueling 6 years. During those 6 years, he never regained his ability to speak coherently or to walk. The old man waited impatiently for his death while Juliet waited impatiently for her freedom. The skeletal hand of the Grim Reaper would be cruel to both.

Bennett then placed the pen in his father's barley functioning hand. His eyes were open, yet unseeing. Bennett took his father's hand and helped him make his mark on the Articles. It was nothing more than a shaky, child like "X" but a mark that would once again change forever the lives of those he had once sought to free. The others sitting around the bed were uncomfortable and had to force themselves to witness their own guilt. The Articles had now been signed. Juliet's family had not only lost their freedom, but were now subject to being sold to the highest bidder.

Chapter 8
Hope No Longer

Old man Crafton finally died in August of 1848.

Several weeks went by while Juliet patiently awaited word that she and the others were now free to leave. That word never came.

After 4 weeks of waiting, Juliet went to Bennett and told him, "I know what was in Mr. John's Will! He told me the day he had Mr. Parker come to the house. We was to be free when Mr. Crafton died and he now be dead for 4 whole weeks! Why is we still slaves, Mr. Bennett?"

Bennett angrily replied, "Don't you dare raise your voice to me! If you must know, Mr. *John* changed his mind. You have no say in this matter and you best remember your place, Juliet!"

Juliet could only stare coldly at him. Words were not needed to convey her thoughts on this matter.

Bennett continued, "I told my father that y'all would not take this well and that the best thing he could do would to sell each and everyone of you that were mentioned in his Will. It seems that he was right to take this in consideration!"

Juliet's anger gave way to an intense deflation of spirit. Physically, she felt that she would become ill. Her freedom being stolen by Bennett was one thing. The shocking news that they were to be sold was an entirely different matter. Thoughts of being separated from her family and friends was more than she could endure. Her heart was pounding and suddenly the room was narrowing and her vision restricted. If death was coming for her, then she was ready but just rolling over and dying was not in her nature. She would fight. And she would pray. Surely God would hear her.

Juliet returned to her cramped quarters and prayed until she fell into a restless sleep. When she woke she had to once again face the horrible truth of the day's events. Moses was sitting with her by the bed and she could see that this gentle giant of a man had been crying. Her sleep had been so erratic that he thought that she had gotten a death inducing fever. He did not know that what faced them all now was worse than death. Her second thought was of him, of how she would be able to break the news to him about the second freedom revoking will and the directive in it that required that they all be sold.

Moses may have been physically strong, but his sweet nature did not carry with it an inner strength as was the case with Juliet. Juliet has always been the rock on which the others depended. They always looked to her for wisdom and strength. If she faltered now, she would fail them in ways that she could only imagine. But, what hope could she possibly provide them? Without freedom, she was unable to utilize the tools available to the white man. Her only tool was prayer and there was no way she knew what God had in mind. It was in His hands now.

As she always said to others, *"If you don't jump in the pond, you nevuh gonna swim"* and then repeated or her own sake, *"If* you *don't jump in the pond, you nevuh gonna swim"* With her faith rocked, she now said this to herself. And repeated many times over.

Chapter 9
Hope Rekindled

This moment to "*jump in the pond*" soon arrived. She had been called on to help load the wagon
with supplies from town and was waiting in the wagon while the Russell family (they no longer went by Crafton in any form) socialized with others who had come to town. They, like others in town, would catch up on the goings on in the county, catching the latest gossip and providing some of their own when Juliet heard her named being called.

"Juliet? Juliet!"

Juliet turned towards the voice, surprised that anyone would call her name, much less know her name.

"Juliet, you may not remember me. My name is Richard Parker and I wrote Mr. Crafton's will for him."

Juliet responded, "Yes, suh. I's member you. What's it you want of me?"

"Been thinking of that will I wrote for Mr. John Russell Crafton that had provided for your freedom and then hearing later that another document *supposedly* written and signed by Mr. Crafton revoked your freedom. Is this true, Juliet?"

"If it weren't true, Mr. Parker, I can tell you for sure, I wouldn't be sitting in this here wagon still a slave. It weren't right, Mr Parker. It weren't right at all."

"That's why I want to talk to you. Something actually doesn't seem right." he replied with one eye brow arched.

Juliet replied cautiously and with not without a small amount of curiosity, "The Craftons...um I mean Russells, they be coming along soon. Don't think I should be talkin' with you. They ain't gonna like seein' me talkin' with you. You might kinda conjure up things in their heads that they just as soon not want to face"

Parker stroked his clean shaven chin and thought this over for a brief moment. He then replied, "Let me handle that. You have a nice day Miss Juliet. We'll talk later. That I can assure you."

Parker knew more than he let on to Juliet. He himself had filed Crafton's will and had been informed that several days later, Bennett had come to the court house and filed a second will. A will that had obviously not been drawn up by an attorney. No attorney worth his salt would have left out the critical statement that all subsequent wills would have had included in it. *I revoke all previous wills and codicils......* The will Bennett filed did not include this language and *this* would be the cornerstone on which he would build his case, but certainly not the entirety of the case. A foundation must be laid to accommodate a cornerstone and he was already visualizing the foundation.

Richard Parker scanned the streets of Berryville for any sign of Bennett, or anyone who might know his whereabouts. Berryville was a typical small town in Virginia where residences and shops randomly shifted from the elegant to primitive. During heavy rains, the streets became a quagmire, mixed with mud and animal waste, topped with a random garnish of rotting vegetables carelessly thrown from windows as if the rain would somehow devour them. In general, people accepted these conditions as a part of life. People have a way of becoming accustomed to that which they have known all their life and most have scant experiences in which to compare. In 1848, most people seldom left the borders of their small county.

What the town did have were all the basic businesses in which to serve their patron's immediate needs. Those businesses included several general stores that competed within rock throwing distance of one another, a doctor's office, a courthouse, a blacksmith's shop, liveries, taverns and lawyer offices. The lawyer offices nearly out numbered the taverns, and this was no mean feat. It was said that the first structure in the little town was a tavern and had been so successful that a demand for more was only limited by the supply of alcohol available. So it would be natural that taverns and law offices formed an oddly symbiotic relationship with taverns that provided unintentional clients for the lawyers. Liquor induced disputes in these taverns would often lead to arrest, and those arrested would often have to seek out the services of a lawyer. Both lawyers and taverns got a piece of a pie that was endlessly passed around the table.

Bar fighting was an honored tradition in old Battle Town, (the earlier name for Berryville that was still used by most citizens), with the town's most celebrated personage considered the father of local tavern bawling. Gen. Daniel Morgan of Revolutionary War fame lived on the outskirts of Berryville and had become a legend in that first early tavern. It was still debated as to whether he went to the tavern to drink or went to the tavern to fight. What was known was that he prepared in advance for a fight by leaving piles of stones strategically placed from his home to the tavern so that as he retreated from tavern with a number of men in hot pursuit, he could stop at his rock pile arsenals and unleash a barrage of stones at his pursuers, thus keeping them at bay.

Drunkenness had no societal boundaries and it was not unusual for the lawyer to represent a client for disorderly conduct as a result of drunkenness and then represent himself for the same charge minutes later. Parker was not one of these lawyers. It wasn't that he was against strong drink. He merely didn't care for the taste.

Parker suddenly spotted Bennett walking out of one of the general stores with a grain bag on each shoulder. His knee high black boots were worn but made of quality leather. His britches were coarse and durable, made for practicality rather than for appearance. Underneath his black vest and long black coat was a clean white shirt buttoned to the neck. He seldom wore a hat except when in the fields, and today was no exception. His long hair was thick with a color darker than a rainy moonless night. The only gray in his hair was oddly enough on just one side of his head and gave him the appearance that someone had brushed a two inch wide swath of white paint from the part at the top of his head to the tips of his hair. Like most people of that time, his eyes were blue, but unlike most people, the blue had an intensity that was considered by some women to produce within them both a tentativeness and attraction towards him. But to men it was something quite different. To most men, his eyes were no different from any other man's eyes except when provoked. It was at these times that the color of his eyes alter from their normal bright blue to a menacing dark blue. This transformation would give warning much in the same way the rattlers on a snake gave warning.

Berryville, Virginia
circa 1863

Parker was wary of Bennett and knew him to be a tough business minded man. He had single handily built up his farm and was determined to expand his holdings at every opportunity. He was not a mean spirited man, but he would stand his ground when necessary. If there had been any doubt of him not standing his ground, that was erased when he shot and killed a man. As Parker understood it, Bennett had sold a sow to Barr with the promise that Bennett would be paid in a week's time. At the end of a week Barr claimed that the sow had died and he was not going to pay Bennett. Indeed the sow had died but as the story unfolded, word had it that one of Barr's sons had killed the beast for butchering. Witnesses had said that old man Barr was furious with his son, as the sow had been purchased, not for meat, but for breeding. Barr had then come up with the story that the sow had died on it's own accord and he determined not to pay Bennett for the *defective* sow. Bennett and several of his sons had ridden over to Barr's place and confronted him with the facts and told him that he had persons willing to testify that his son had killed the sow who had mistakenly thought it was to be butchered. Bennett had taken his musket with him so as to impress upon Barr that he meant business and that he planned to take him to court if he did not pay up. After a heated argument, Barr turned a began walking away, but he just couldn't leave it alone. He turned and called out to Bennett and pulled an old single shot pistol from his belt and fired. Although, the bullet had missed it's mark, Bennett already had the musket positioned against his shoulder and returned fire. Bennett's ball did not miss it's mark. Barr lingered for little more than a day and died as a result of his wound. In court, Bennett's sons testified as to Bennett's account of the incident and surprisingly, Barr's own son confirmed the story. Bennett was immediately found not guilty of murder. He did not take pride in killing another man, and it quietly weighed on him. He later had another sow with piglets delivered to the Barr farm and placed in an empty sty. Bennett never admitted that he had done such. It would not bring back old man Barr and it did little to help assuage his own guilt but at least he had tried to make amends in his own secretive way. Bennett was not a bad man by any means but nevertheless, he became a man worthy of a certain wary respect after that fateful day, and Parker could be counted among the wary.

Parker caught Bennett exiting one of the general stores and called out, "Mr. Russell! Could I have several minutes of your time, please."

Bennett paused for a moment before replying, "Let me get these grain sacks off my shoulders and into the wagon first."

Parker did not want to be at the wagon where Juliet waited and replied, "I'd be happy to help you to the wagon with your grain bags if you could find the kindness in which to speak with me now. It is quite important and should not wait."

Bennett was on full alert now and tossed the bags from his shoulders to the ground with a dull, heavy thud that sent small clouds of grain dust exploding from the porous, loosely woven bags.

He quickly sized up Parker's need to speak with him here and now instead of following him to the wagon replied, "I assume that since you didn't want to wait until I got to the wagon that this must have something to do with Juliet?" Bennett liked getting right to the point. He had little patience with those who beat around the bush.

Parker knew enough about Bennett to know that it was best to get right to the point, "I'm not going to pussy foot around with you, Bennett. It has everything to do with Juliet. As you know, I had been both a friend and counsel to your father. I have always had the highest respect for Mr. Russell (he thought that there was no need to refer to him by his legal name of Crafton) and for yourself, as well. There has been no time where I did not find any of your family to be anything other than honorable. That said, it had been your father's last will and testament to free Juliet and all the slaves that were personally owned by your father"

Bennett remained quiet and studied Parker as he continued. "So, it came to my surprise when after the passing of Mr. Russell, his slaves had not been freed per his request and desire. Possibly you could enlighten me as to the reasons as to why Mr. Russell's wishes in his last will and testament had not been carried out?"

Bennett did not hesitate replying, "As you are well aware of Mr.

Parker, my father had become quite ill and his health continued to deteriorate. As you would also be aware of, the cost for his care was no little amount of money. He did not want to be a financial burden to his family and desired to find a way as to not become a financial burden on his family as his pride dictated. After some thought on this matter, my father made the decision that his slaves would be hired out so as to offset the costs of his care. So, that there would be no mistaking his wishes he decided to amend his will in a separate paper writing that would be legally binding"

Parker thought this through and then replied, "I have several questions. Although, I fully understand
your father's desire to help in the cost of his continued care, I must ask you why he had not asked for *me* to amend his original will as is usually customary between client and attorney?"

Bennett replied, but his voice betrayed his former confidence, "It had not seemed important that you or any legal assistance whatsoever would be necessary, considering the small change within his will."

Parker was somewhat stunned by Bennett's assertion that the change to the will was *small* and replied, "I fear that you may have left out one important detail, which to those it may effect, would hardly be considered "*a small change.* In addition to the hiring out of the slaves to offset the costs of your father's care, this *other* will -and I hesitate to call it a will- left a directive to sell the slaves upon Mr. Crafton's, or otherwise known as Russell's, death."

Parker saw Bennett blanch and continued. "Exactly how many slaves did your father own? I believe it was 14, but please correct me if I am wrong." No argument was offered regarding the number of slaves and Parker then fired a warning shot across

Bennett's bow by stating, "The sale of these slaves would garnish somewhere between $10,000 and $14,000. A sum of money that many men would not see in a lifetime. You must be quite pleased with this windfall? You need not answer that question, Mr. Russell. There will be plenty of time for that later." Parker casually brushed some non-existent dust from his lapel and stated, "I will be representing Juliet and the others and suggest that you seek counsel as soon as possible. I would also recommend that should Juliet, or any of the others suddenly disappear or are sold, that you could very well be found guilty of obstruction of justice and felonious grand theft."

As Parker turned to walk away he stopped and spun back towards Bennett and said, "Of course, none of this needs to become a long and exorbitant costly trial if Juliet and the others are freed within the next several weeks. I will be filing the suit on behalf of Juliet immediately, but of course if the slaves are freed per Mr. Russell's initial direction in his will, the suit would become moot, thus saving us all time and money. I have seen suits of this nature drag on for years where the eventual selling of the slaves either barely paid for the legal expenses or actually cost the heirs money"

Parker hoped that Bennett would accept the reasonable route and free Juliet and the others. He knew that Bennett would need to discuss this with his brothers and sisters prior to taking action one way or the other, but the money each of the Russell siblings would get in the sale of the slaves would in all likelihood beckon to them like a sirens song. Parker knew that his case would all hinge on how he presented it. There were a number of avenues he could pursue and the least of which would be to show the heirs as being willing victims of good old fashion greed. Another tactic would be to prove that the purported second will had been either been entirely fraudulent or to show that John Russell had been coerced to sign or more likely he was not of sound mind when he did sign. Greed was easy to show but it had no true legal weight. Proving fraud or unsoundness of mind that relied on fuzzy memories from 6 years ago would be difficult, if not impossible. He would have to sow doubt in the jury's mind regarding this suspicious paper writing amending the original will, such as it is, and to utilize the vagaries of the law itself to sway both judge and jury. He had much work to do before going to court.

Before Richard Parker left to walk away, he said, "Bennett? I believe I offered to help you carry your grain bags to the wagon."

Bennett's eyes darkened and no words were necessary to reply to Parker's offer. The answer was wordless yet there was no misunderstanding.

Parker ended with, "I shall visit with Miss Juliet Sunday after next and I am most assured that your subscription to the honorable ways of your station and to your long time respect of the righteousness of our country's laws, you will approve of my visit with my client without resorting to court order."

Bennett, not wanting to show concern answered, "By all means. Sunday after next, it is."

Richard E. Parker, Jr.

Chapter 10
Parker Meets With Juliet

Sunday after next had arrived. Parker agilely dismounted from his chestnut mare with the blaze face and three white socks. The horse was fit...proven by it's dappling. Bennett Russell, among other endeavors, bred horses and was known for his keen eye of horse flesh. He had on more than one occasion remarked about the quality of Parker's mare and had even inquired whether Parker would entertain breeding his mare to his top stallion. There had been casual talk regarding this union, but nothing had come of it, and he supposed that there may not be any further talk on that topic today....or at any other time in the future. A shame really. Certainly a foal from this union would have been quite sought after and fetched an excellent price.

"Good morning, Bennett. I pray all is well with you and your family."

Bennett civilly replied, "All, to my most recent knowledge, are doing quite well, thank you. And, I pray all is well with you and your family."

Parker replied, "Indeed it is. Would it be suitable for me to meet with Miss Juliet out by that large chestnut next to your carriage house if it so pleases you?"

"Indeed, Sir. I will summon Juliet for you. She is just finishing up a chore and will be with you as soon as she has completed her task."

As Parker waited, he thought how his meeting with Juliet might raise her hopes too high so he would have to be sure she understood the risk of possible failure. This case would undoubtedly be full of hearsay and witnesses that had much to gain and equally, much to lose. His client, regardless of the facts, was a slave. This put him at a clear disadvantage with a jury, made up of not of her peers, but a jury of Bennett's peers. He had to find a way to keep the jury from seeing color. He probably had a better chance of making a silk purse out of a sow's ear.

While Parker waited, he spied several cut sections of logs that had for the time, avoided being split for firewood. These log sections would serve as seats for the both of them and then arranged them to the side of the carriage house so as not to be in view of the house. Once the primitive seating arrangement had been made, he stepped out from around the carriage house so that he would be seen by Juliet when she came from the house.

Nearly 30 minutes had passed when Juliet became visible walking towards the carriage house. There was something different about this woman that he couldn't put his finger on. She was dressed like all slave women in the most basic of clothing and shoes. Nothing unusual there, but suddenly he knew what it was. Most slaves when approaching a white man would hold their gaze to the ground like a scolded dog. Juliet walked with her head up. Was it pride? If so, would this add to his difficulties in representing her? What would undoubtedly be perceived as an act of an uppity negro would make it all but impossible for him to win over the jury. Pride or not, she would need to act more humble in the face of 12 white jurors and not to mention, the public at large. He would need to be delicate in addressing this issue and make sure she understood how people made judgments on the most minuscule of things, no matter how unreasonable they may be. Pride in a negro was no minuscule infraction of behavior in the Southern society of 1848. He had heard of some slave owners whipping a slave into unconsciousness for just that reason.

Parker greeted Juliet and asked her to have a seat, apologizing for the crude seating arrangement. He knew it wasn't necessary to apologize but wanted her to know that he treated her the same as he would with any client, regardless of color. A good lawyer always wanted his client relaxed and once they were relaxed, communication between lawyer and client can begin in earnest.

Before Juliet could speak Parker said, "How are your husband Moses and your children faring?" Parker knew that any woman, no matter the color, were always be open to conversation about their children. Their husbands, not so much. Parker continued with, "...and what ages are the children now? As a child I would explore caves on the farm, much to my mother's distress. Do you have caves around here?"

He purposely asked one question behind the other to get her talking about her children, with the hope that it would begin to develop the trust and communication that would be needed in the days ahead.

Juliet replied, "They's all doing fine, Mister Parker." She hesitated for a moment and Parker sat quietly and then she added, "Chiluns can be a handful and I guess like all of chiluns, they get into trouble, but it is the way we's all grow, I spose. My boy Marshall seems to grow more than most in that regard! He is what you say, an indeepenent" chile. He's a good boy but just can't seem to sit still and always lookin' for the next thing to do before he finish the first thing. He ain't learned patience, yet."

Richard Parker and Juliet sat for at least an hour just talking about growing up, the joys and frustrations of being a parent. A bond of sorts was beginning to develop between them and it was now time to shift subjects to the primary reason that both knew was the real reason he had come.

With a small break in the conversation, Parker spoke, "I have been making inquiries into the health and soundness of mind of Mr. Crafton when these papers were signed that revoked your and your family's proposed freedom. Keep in mind that it has been 6 years since he signed these so called Articles of Agreement and therefore, memories more times than not, cannot be fully relied upon to recall the facts as they may have actually been at the time. Nevertheless, I have good reason to believe that Mr. Crafton was neither of sound mind or body, when the signed the Articles of Agreement. Sources, who would be in a position to know Mr. Crafton's condition around the time in question, have said to others that they wouldn't have thought Mr. Crafton to have been physically able to have signed these Articles of Agreement, much less sound enough of mind to have known what he was signing."

Parker let that sink in with Juliet and waited to hear her account of Mr. Crafton's condition at the time he purportedly signed the Articles. She was around him everyday and would know better than anyone his true condition at any given time. If it came to court, her testimony would not be able to be heard as slaves did not have the right to do so in a Virginia court of law. What he wanted was to see was if her story of the events of that time reflected the stories he had heard regarding Mr. Crafton's condition. If she could provide one specific trait of his condition that then could be compared to others who saw him near the same time frame, he would know that he could rely on Juliet's account and use it to his advantage. He hadn't worked out those particular details yet, but he was sure that time would provide him with a detailed and organized legal strategy.

Juliet seemed somewhat wary of having a candid conversation with a white man who also happened to be a slave owner, but it wasn't time for second guessing. So, she began relating to Parker her recollections.

"I be with Mr. Crafton since I was just a little girl. Ain't saying we didn't have our run ins. He could be bull headed from time to time, but then, so could I. In time we came to an understandin'. All and all, he was a decent man. When his woman died, he sort of started to rely on me to fill that hole. I don't mean that in a way that a man and woman do in their beds, but in them other ways. Cookin', carin' for him when he got sick and plain keepin' him from lettin' his bullheadedness get in the way of doin' the right thing wid his bizness. He make money that put food on his plate, that same money then put food on my plate. He don't make money, then we all go hungry. It be simple as that."

Parker let Juliet continue to talk, but when she got to when Crafton became ill, how it seemed to have effected him and who else may have witnessed these changes in the old man, Parker's attention to Juliet was now full on.

Juliet continued, "Mister Crafton took ill one day maybe 6 years ago I reckon. I's found him sittin' in a chair with this far away look in his eyes and one side of his face seemed to not match up wit the other side. He couldn't walk or lift one of his arms. It be like half his body just up and died. When he tried to talk it be like his mouth was full of grits. Couldn't hardly make out a word he was sayin'. Dey say now that he had sumpin called stroke. Nasty thing, dat stroke sickness. When you could unerstan'words he be saying, it was all befuddled like and sounded like jibberjabber. It be like he wernt of this world no more, but a world long gone. He be callin' me Ann, his chiluns names I ain't even ever heard of before or he looked at dem like he ain't never seen dem befo. He be in bad shape, Mister Parker, and it only got worse as the years went on."

Parker then asked, "Did Bennett, or any of his brothers and sisters, know that Mr. Crafton had planned to free you all upon his death?"

Juliet pondered for a moment and replied, "I can't' rightly say, but Mister Crafton would time to time, say dat it just don't seem right that one man should own another man. He kinda beat around de bush and when he did, Mister Bennett would say, 'right or not, it's the way it is and de farm don't just run on love. I spect dat dey know what go on in Mr. Crafton's head."

"I suspect you may be right on that point, Juliet", Parker said.

Parker then added, "Did you see Bennett, or anyone else, get Mr. Crafton to sign any papers around that same time he had suffered a stroke?"

Juliet turned away and it was obvious that she was uncomfortable with this question but quietly answered, "I didn't see nothin' but one night while I was cleanin' up after dinner, Mister Bennett, Mister Tom and Mister John and sum man I ain't neva seen befo' walked into Mr. Crafton's bedroom. Dey weren't their long and when dey walked out, Mister Bennett was foldin' a paper and then stuffed it into a pocket inside his coat. De whole thing seemed strange. Nobody said nothin' and all of dem looked like a pack of chiluns' up to no good wit guilty looks on their faces. Mister Bennett then said good night to them all and out of the corner of my eye, I see Mister Bennett gimme a quick look and then he walked out to de front porch and just stood there starin' off to de mountains. Whatever happened in that room weighed heavy on each of them. Dat is, all but that man I nevuh done seen befo'. Wernt no weight on dat man's shoulders. He just walked out and got on some ole mule and rode away. Ain't nevuh seen him since."

Juliet then added, "If dem people all witnessed Mr. John's will, don't it strike you odd dat everyone in dat room dat night had sumthin' to get out of all dis? But, de stranger ain't family, so what he get out of de deal? Dat man need to be found and mo likely than not, he need to be flushed out like a rat in de kitchen pantry. I 'spect dat Mr. Bennet need someone other than family to sign on dis will and be no surprise to me that he be paid to do that. And if he be paid to lie, then he be a person who probly' have skeletons in his closet. Dem skeletons could be used to make dis man squeal like a pig!"

Parker was astonished that Juliet had so quickly arrived at the same conclusion as himself regarding the makeup of the witnesses to the second will. The question she composed about the stranger was indeed a mystery. *What did this stranger get out of all this?* Parker's admiration for Juliet's ability to see flaws in the second will and then point them out, had just risen to such a level that he was beginning to see her more as a partner than a client. She was able to see through the smoke screens and make proper deductions. In another world and in another time, he very well could see himself standing across from her in a courtroom arguing a case. She would have been a formidable opponent! Of that, he had no doubt. He hadn't thought about the fact that he may very well need to find bait to flush the stranger out of his hole and that he may have an unsavory past and history with the law. He now had more reason to listen to Juliet, other than her reciting of her memory of events.

Parker stood up and said, "The fact that I had recorded the original will first puts the burden of proof upon Mr. Russell. That is to say, he must challenge the original will and we must defend that original will. In an odd way, the burden falls more upon us, as we must attempt to show that this so called second will is not only technically incorrect, but for all practical purposes, we must show that this second will of his is rife with fraud. No easy task, and in just alluding to such a criminal action will create extreme tensions that may not be in the least bit pleasant for either one of us."

Parker knew that Juliet had never seen the will Bennett recorded, but it told him that Juliet had been truthful about the evening Bennett had Mr. Crafton sign another will. The will Bennett recorded had four names on it that witnessed the signing. Bennett, Tom, John and one unknown man by the name of Spurr. Where this unknown man lived, Parker didn't know, but he knew he did not live in their small county of Clarke. He would have to find out where this man lived. What his connection to Bennett was and as to the character of this man. His defense of Juliet and the will was beginning to fall into place. He mounted his horse feeling more confident than when he arrived. As he wheeled his horse around towards the road home, he caught sight of Bennett standing quietly and alone on his front porch with his eyes resting upon Parker. He did not detect any fear in Bennett's eyes and did not expect to see fear. If anything, Bennett's eyes showed a calm determination. Parker knew that Bennett would not break under court room examination. His brother Tom and his son John would waiver but they would do as Bennett instructed them to do. They would wobble, but not fall. He needed to find this man they called Spurr. And as Juliet said, he may need to be *flushed out* and then under intense examination, make this old boy—as Juliet said-- *squeal.*

Before Parker departed, he turned to Juliet and said, "I almost forgot. I have a small gift for you." He reached into his jacket pocket and produced a bright red scarf which he handed to Juliet. She looked down at the scarf and then shyly raised her head. Then with an ever broadening smile on her face, both hands reached out and took the scarf with the delicacy of a child holding her first butterfly.

"Thank you so very much for your time and understanding, Juliet." Parker mounted his horse and rode out of the farm and onto the old Alexandria Road that would take him back to his home along the Shenandoah River and Blue Ridge Mountains.

Chapter 11
The Trial's Opening Arguments– May 1848

Parker and Juliet entered the white columned, brick courthouse where the jury, who had been chosen at an earlier session, had already assembled. The makeup of the jury was to be expected. White, male, prosperous and last, but not least, slave owners. Many of the faces that sat in the jury box this day were recognizable. Henry Washington, James Larue, John Pierce, Carter Shepherd, to just name a few. Parker took a seat at the table provided for defense just off to the side where the judge would be preside from his lofty perch above them all. Juliet took a seat behind Parker. As a slave, she could not join Parker at the table. Although, she had rights, they were limited. The chair provided for her was placed in the darkest corner of the courtroom. With her dark complexion, she had in essence disappeared. A not so subtle reminder of her limitations as a slave.

The court room was designed to allow a northern light to be cast on the judge from a large window directly behind him. The sunlight that filtered through was more haze than light which gave the presiding judge a *reverent* quality. Those who had felt the court's wrath might say that the judge had more of a *revenant like* quality. The other large window allowed for southern light to be cast upon all those in attendance. Having a large southern window allowed for the court room to be lit regardless of the time of the year without the harshness of direct lighting. A small balcony ran across one side of the court room where more seating was located if needed. Today, the balcony was indeed needed and overflowed with curious onlookers, hecklers and entertainment seekers. The courtroom itself took on the odor of the unwashed, the damp beginnings of mildew and a passing scent of lilac that women brought with them in a vain attempt to fight off the first two odors. For those who arrived too late, they milled around any open window struggling to hear snippets of the activity inside. They needn't worry. There would be more hearings. Hearings that would take 8 long years.

Low murmurs from several hundred people in the court was suddenly interrupted with the words, "All rise! The court is now in session, the honorable Judge J. R. Douglas presiding."

The formality of the court and the crowds gathered at the courtroom trying to get a glimpse of Juliet, made her wish that the chair she sat in would retreat further into the dark alcoves of the courtroom. It didn't. So she sat erect. Nervously defiant. She knew that her defiance would not win her any sympathy, but she was not here for sympathy. She was here for her freedom and the freedom of her family. She would not grovel for freedom. Freedom was for those who took it. Not for those who bowed down.

When the judge took his seat, the bailiff then cried out, "All be seated." As if on cue, the murmuring of the audience began in full force once again, but the judge brought down his gavel with the force of a guillotine and authoritatively stated, "Order in the court! All of those who do not remain orderly will be removed from my court immediately and taken to the jail to be tried at a later date for contempt of court!" A hush fell over the crowd. As much as they wanted to talk among themselves, their desire to be entertained at this proceeding was even greater. None wanted to miss today's show *sitting in a jail cell.*

The judge now announced, "In the case of Bennett Russell and Others vs. Negroes Juliet and Others, this court is now in session.

The plaintiffs attorney will now approach the bench and present their case."

Bennett had acquired the services of a local attorney named Philip Williams. He was by nature a nervous man, but when walked into a courthouse, a dramatic transformation took place. The courtroom floor was his stage and it was there that he felt most comfortable. Physically, he was described in local vernacular, a *tall drink of water.* Everything about him was thin. His face. His nose. His lips. His fingers. Everything. His dress was not neat and precise, but neither was it slovenly in appearance. Due to his height and thinness, his pants always appeared to have been made specifically for wading through high water. All and all, a fairly unremarkable man, but what God takes away, He giveth in another way. In this case God had given Williams a rich baritone which he used to great effect in a courtroom. If his physical features were considered sharp, then so too was his mind. Other attorneys who had only met him in a setting other than a courtroom, had always underestimated him. A mistake that they would not ever repeat again.

Williams, awkward just an hour before, but now comfortably in his milieu, walked gracefully and slowly along the front of the jury box, making eye contact with each one and lingering just a brief moment more on those who he had earlier chosen as jurors and accepted by the defense.

The attorney for the plaintiff kept it simple. He argued that since the first will had been written in 1839 and the second will written in 1842, then it would stand to reason that the latter will would be the true last will and testament of John Russell Crafton by the mere fact that it was the most recent will. He further reminded the judge and the jury that a man had the right to change his mind and write a second will that reflected his wishes of that moment in his life. He reminded the jury that this happened in more cases than not. In some cases, he wished to change his executor. Or wished to disown an heir or add someone to their will. Or to change the basic intentions of a will. That amending a will was as natural as a flowing stream that over time continues to change courses. He further reminded the jury that each one of us has changed their mind a thousand times, over their lifetime, on a multitude of issue and that changes in a will were no different, other than it was put in writing. Therefore the changing of Mr. Crafton's mind was nothing more than that. A change of his mind. Legal in all regards and not to be questioned by others. Williams rich, deep baritone voice neared a crescendo as he scolded society for even considering this case worthy of a court's time. He scolded those who would disagree with him. Scolded Juliet. Scolded her attorney and would have scolded the judge for even bothering taking the bench today, had he not thought the wiser of such.

After offering the Articles of Agreement for probate which was accompanied by nearly one hour of an opening argument that was constructed more on emotion than the law, it nevertheless, had it's desired effect. Most did not need to be convinced of the right of a man to keep and sell slaves should he so desire, but he had wanted to arouse those feelings of superiority when it became time for the jury to render a verdict. Williams had played to the jury's most basic instincts. William's tactic was as simple as it was elegant. Appeal to the most basic prejudices of the jurors and don't confuse them with the complexities of the law. The judge would not agree with such a tactic, but then, as Phillips was well aware, the judge would not be rendering a decision. The jury would.

Parker would not show his entire hand today, knowing that the court would be continued to the next regularly schedules hearing in 6 months time. The judge would never ask the jury to sequester for a finding on nothing but opening argument. When it was time for the jury to make a decision, he knew the judge would give instructions and remind the jury of the laws that governed a jury's decision.. Therefore, Parker had decided to use the law to sway both the judge and jury.

The judge then called on Parker to give his opening statement.

"Your honor and gentlemen of the jury, there are a number of reasons I can give that can cast more than a little doubt on the validity of the second will that has since been titled as the Articles of Agreement, but for now, I will demonstrate to the court just two of the reasons that this case against my client should be dismissed and done so with all haste. If indeed this second will is an agreement, then should it not by definition be a contract between two or more parties? And if so, then why indeed would these Articles of Agreement be entered as the final will and testament of Mr. Crafton and not more appropriately as a contract that should have been entered as such in 1842 when signed? Instead, the plaintiff's attorney is attempting to make each of you believe that a dog is really a cat. This insults the intelligence of the court, the jurors and every man and woman here today! But for argument sake lets just assume for the moment that the *Articles of Agreement* is considered to be the last will and testament of John Russell Crafton.

Philip Williams

I have had the Articles of Agreement transcribed and with the permission of the court, I would like to enter them into evidence as Exhibit 1. I have transcribed an additional 12 copies which I would like to now pass out to the jury. I ask each of the jurors to read through the Articles of Agreement and to please take your time."

After about 10 minutes, each juror looked up, indicating that they had read the Articles of Agreement. Parker then proceeded.

"Gentlemen of the jury, I have but one simple question of you.

Do these Articles of Agreement state anywhere that this said paper writing hereby revokes any previous wills or codicils before it?"

The jury did not expect to be quizzed on the content of the Articles of Agreement and therefore the heads of each juror suddenly dropped down to the paper in their hand and began searching the Articles like a classroom of young students desperate to find the answer to their teacher's question.

Parker again stated, "Gentlemen, please take all the time you like and then indicate that you have read the paper writing to your individual satisfaction. There is no time limit placed on the eventuality of justice. Justice, my esteemed gentlemen, may be blind to whether one be rich or poor, but she needs your eyes today to help guide her. So please, once again, take all the time required by you."

Certainly a simple request, but this time the jury members took even more time to read and then re-read the Articles of Agreement. No one wanted to be the classroom dunce and were taking no chances that they would be the only one to answer incorrectly and thus, the object of ridicule. When they had completed their assigned task, one by one they lifted their eyes from the paper to indicate that they had indeed read carefully every word and now knew the answer to Parker's question.

Parker then went down the line, juror by juror, asking the same question he had asked them earlier. Had they seen *anywhere* in this so called Articles of Agreement if there had been any statement in it which revoked any previous will or codicil? Most of the jurors answered with a simple "NO." Two of the jurors, understanding his clever tactic, avoided the simple yes or no answer, began to speak, but Parker cut them off quickly and reminded them that by the very nature of the question that there could not be any answer, other than yes or no.

Parker's tactic of asking the jury this question was twofold. First and foremost, he had planted the seed that the Articles did not revoke any previous will and as time went on, he would feed that seed and watch it grow. Secondly, it helped flush out those jurors he suspected of making a decision in favor of the Articles before they had even been sworn in. Every jury has those who have predetermined the outcome. For those jurors who do not fall favorably into your own corner, it is the job of an attorney to place doubt in the minds of those jurors. To make them think as you wish them to think. To nudge them along without their noticing. Once you know which juror or jurors will be difficult, the attorney can begin to groom them by appealing to their ego. This tactic is varied, subtle and at times have the complexity of a palace intrigue. Great politicians have used similar methods to convert their greatest detractors to their greatest supporters. A courtroom is as much about the minds of men as it is about the law. Plant the seed. Let it grow. Convert weeds to flowers.

Clarke County Courthouse
Berryville, Virginia
Established 1838

Once each juror finally answered that there was nothing in the Articles of Agreement that said it revoked any or all wills or codicils that may have preceded the Articles. Satisfied with the results of his first volley, Parker walked confidently and slowly back to the table that served as his courtroom desk. His slow pace back to his table was calculated so as to allow the conclusion that the said Articles of Agreement had not *legally* revoked the original will to further invade the psyche of the jurors, courtroom gawkers and most importantly, Judge Douglas. The judge would obviously understand the minutiae of the law and would be required to direct the jurors in regard to such before the jury sequestered for a verdict.

Before Parker turned to sit down, he caught Juliet's eye and gave her a nearly imperceptible nod but there was no hiding a mischievous like twinkle in his eyes. It was moments like these that made the tedium of law all worthwhile. He knew that the plaintiff's attorney, had for the moment, been knocked off balance. Today's court was intended for just opening arguments. A chance to strut the stage like an actor on opening night. In reality, lawyers were actors who just happened to read law.

The judge could see the excitement building in the throngs of people who had come to see a show and Act 1 had not disappointed. The old judge had been around long enough to understand the telltale signs that led to disruption in his courtroom by the attending public. He had no desire to throw any of the public in jail for disorderly conduct. Once a judge goes down that road, it can mushroom into either passive consent to orderly behavior or rejection by the public, leading to near riotous behavior. To maintain control of a courtroom without the risk involved, it was sometimes wiser to just call it a day. And he did just that. His gavel rang out like a shot bringing the crowds full attention to the judge's stern face. He paused for several seconds to allow for today's attendee's to scold their neighbors with pokes from their elbows who had seemingly been deaf and ignorant to the judge's attempt to regain order in his court. When the court finally calmed, the old judge's scowling face bore into the guilty faces of the audience for several long seconds before he sat back in his chair and spoke.

"Opening statements by both attorneys have been made and noted. Court is hereby adjourned until the next term." The judge once again struck his gavel and rose to leave, while at the same time the din of voices rose to deafening levels. The only disappointment the public had was the 6 month wait for Act II. Circuit courts met only twice a year. No one suspected that this human drama would become a series of continuations, postponements and recesses that would drag on for years to come.

Parker would have time to prepare his next phase of the argument but, so would Philip Williams.

Parker needed to keep Williams off balance and only an offensive tactic could accomplish that. Williams had already been put on the defensive and although, he would expect Parker to continue an offensive, he would not know how he would be attacked. This would give Parker the advantage if properly planned and he had 6 months in which to prepare and make subtle feints by dropping well placed rumors, with the hope of baiting Williams into preparing for that which would never happen. Battles are often won by luring your enemy into a trap. The question was, would the trap hold it's prey?

Both Parker and Bennett has surmised that the courtroom today would draw large crowds. And both were keenly aware that large crowds were just a breath away from becoming an unruly mob. Therefore, they had taken the precaution to have Juliet exit out of the courtroom's back door and be met by one of Bennett's sons with a wagon to carry Juliet home, taking the back way out of town. Parker walked with Juliet through the hallway to the rear exit. She had not understood the attorney's when they had used Latin phrases to explain certain elements of the law, but she understood the essence of the arguments each attorney had made. She understood that freedom would not come swiftly, but instead, with a painful slowness.

Parker helped her into the back of the wagon where she sat with her legs dangling over the edge, and her red scarf wound carefully around her head. He watched as they pulled away. Although Juliet was relegated to the back of the wagon, she held herself erect like some Nubian princess he had once read about. It was not so much deliberate pride, as it was an unconscious and natural way with her. He couldn't help to wonder about this woman's African roots. He had met men who had little to show for their life, but their surname and their carriage suggested that somewhere in their ancestry there had been more. Parker suspected that Juliet may be one of these family members who fate had dealt them a losing hand, but that they hadn't always held a losing hand.

No doubt that the future will also hold a similar fate for his own descendants, he thought. History has shown that wealth and power ebbs and flows within a family. Like streams branching off into other streams, the parent stream loses it strength and power, while the new branches either grow in size or come to an abrupt end, sinking below the surface.

Chapter 12
The Attempted Rape

The days passed slowly for Juliet. Expectation and impatience has a way of retarding time. It would be nearly 5 months before court was held again, and her patience was as thin and brittle as a skin of ice on a shallow pond.

To make things worse, Jenkins, the overseer of the farm, had been leering more than usual at her daughter, Harriet, who was only 12 years old at the time, but it could easily be seen that she was becoming not only a woman, but a woman of rare beauty. The man would need watching. The devil was in that man and his fondness for whiskey made for a nasty combination. Saturday nights was Jenkins time to drink and today was Thursday. Yes. He would indeed need watching!

It was late Saturday night when she heard Jenkins' wagon creaking past the main house where Moses and she lived in part of the semi detached summer kitchen. She heard him curse when the wagon dropped hard in one of the many pot holes in the road. The man's lungs seemed to be forever full of phlegm like some injured tree oozing sap. Juliet heard him coughing, followed by the inevitable clearing of the phlegm that flew from his mouth like the afterbirth of a mother cow. She shuddered just thinking about it.

Harriet's quarters were approximately 200 feet away from her own. Normally, there would be others with her but Mister Bennett had hired out those who would normally be there to protect her. She was alone and Jenkins was drunk. Hopefully he would get to his house and pass out as he normally did and cause no trouble tonight.

Jenkins staggered to his door and once inside plopped himself down in an old wooden chair that had been made by Moses. Harriet was on his mind. The thoughts he had were lewd....even by his standards. He closed his eyes, enjoying his own lewdness, but he had drank heavily that night and it wasn't long before he fell into a deep drunken slumber.

Thunder slowly rolled in the distance to the west where summer storms were given birth. The summer storms would gather in strength and ferocity as they began to mix with the cooler mountain air sweeping down from the east. Rock Hall, Bennett Russell's farm, was often the storm's bulls eye where the warm and cool air collided. It had been several hours since Jenkins had lost consciousness and he was still in his chair when a crack of lightning hit somewhere close to his tenant quarters. Lightning bolts were now being hurled angrily towards Earth as if God was creating a new chapter to the bible. The viciousness of the storm could wake the dead and Jenkins started so violently that he fell out his improvised bed, striking his head against the table. The fog of whiskey was quickly being lifted by the sharp and sober inducing pain in his head. When the pain subsided his consciousness found it's way back to Harriet. He was now wide awake and was determined to feed his lust.

Dressed in a canvas slicker coated in a thin layer of boiled fat and a crumpled black hat pulled down to just above his eyes, he huddled within his coat against the elements and began his clandestine mission towards the quarters of Harriet. He knew she would be alone, since it was he who had taken the other slaves to be hired out to their appointed destinations. His primitive cabin was about one half mile from where Harriet was sleeping. He roughly calculated it would take about 15 minutes of slogging through the rain and mud to make it to his destination of debauchery. Harriet's bed.

Jenkins slowly opened the door to Harriet's quarters and confirmed that she was alone, *asleep and….. vulnerable.* He moved silently to her bed.

As he stood over her, he anxiously unbuckled his belt and dropped his pants to his knees. As he fell upon Harriet, she woke with a start and a raspy growl was emitted from this creature of the dark. The sound she heard was a voice that now threateningly told her to remain quiet or that her throat would be slit from ear to ear while he took the dull side of his knife and traced a line slowly across her neck. His breath smelled of pungent disease and cheap whiskey. This alone so nauseated Harriet that she actually felt the bile quickly rising in her throat and burning the passageway raw.

Jenkins then put his hand up Harriet's dress he began forcing her legs open. She let out a scream that was quickly muffled by Jenkins' calloused and filthy hand. He briefly removed his hand, only to strike Harriet sharply across the face. The forceful slap to Harriet served not only the purpose of quieting her but by inflicting pain on his victim, it aroused his bent and twisted mind. Her lip split open in two separate places, but she was immune to the pain. The pain had been replaced with a numbing fear and shock of having this befouled creature writhing on her like some great poisonous serpent that had slithered from it's lair.

Juliet had not rested well on this night, or any other night for that matter. She had been worried about Harriet and coupled with the storm, she was awake and alert, even to the secondary sounds that still existed between the clap of thunder and lightning. The scream was short and nearly drowned out by the heavy drops of rain, but Juliet's sharpened senses of worry still heard a short desperate cry and feared the worse. She rushed out into the darkness and steady downpour, heading for Harriet's quarters with a sense of dread.

When Juliet arrived at Harriet's, the door was swinging open from the whipping winds that accompanied the storm. What she saw was Jenkins straddling the legs of the twelve year old Harriet and grunting like some old rutting boar hog. Had it not been for the specter of freedom, she would have grabbed the heavy cast iron skillet and turned Jenkins head to mush. She had to stop Jenkins but she had to somehow push away the wild animal instincts that had risen up within her. Killing Jenkins would bring to an end her dream of freedom. A murderess, especially a black murderess, would be hanged in short order. It was unfortunate, she thought, that freedom would get in the way of killing such vermin.

Nevertheless, she grabbed the skillet and brought it down hard on his pockmarked buttocks. Jenkins let out some unearthly sound and quickly spun off of Harriet. His watery, bloodshot eyes were filled with hatred and reactive revenge.

Juliet stood her ground and shouted, "Git the Hell out of here! Now!"

Jenkins stared and then gave a loud false laugh saying, "And what the hell is some black *bitch* gonna do? Grab me and throw me out?"

Juliet was calm considering the situation, but replied, "I don't have to throw out no white trash. Mister Bennett will do that for me and you ain't neva git no job in these parts ever again."

Jenkins said nothing at first. He knew that Bennett Russell, although a slave owner himself, had repeatedly made clear, that anyone who harmed his slaves in anyway whatsoever, were in fact harming his business and therefore in turn, harming him. Some slave owners were cruel, but Russell was not one of them. It wasn't as if he was enlightened, he just looked at slaves as a piece of machinery or chattel that required proper handling if one was to expect it to perform to it's maximum level of efficiency. Russell was a businessman first and foremost. It wasn't that he didn't have empathy for the conditions of others. It just wasn't his primary motivation. Bennett has seen other men who sexually and physically abused their slaves and saw how the effectiveness of a slave was diminished. A contented slave always outperformed the non-contented, and contentment, in his mind, equated to profit. Jenkins knew that Russell would see his actions as both a disruption of efficiency and a personal affront to him. Although Jenkins may have been cruel, and slow to figure out the simplest of tasks, he wasn't slow when it came to understanding that his job would be terminated and that he had few, if any prospects for future employment elsewhere in the county. For now, he would remain quiet and return to his cabin.

Jenkins was seething as he walked towards the door and his combination of hatred for Juliet and at his own embarrassment for backing down exploded as he neared Juliet. His fist struck Juliet so hard that her head kicked back like the recoil of a shotgun. Juliet fell to her knees, but rather than cower, she was frothing with rage. It took everything she had to remain on the floor, bowed before Jenkins, but too much was at stake to act rashly. Before Jenkins had turned the corner to walk home, she was already developing her plan to get even. She would need help

and knew exactly where to look for her accomplices. The farm
had many small wooded areas with rock outcroppings. It was
there that her accomplices lived.

   The one thing that Juliet could take comfort from on this
unspeakable night was that Jenkins had been too drunk to get an
erection and therefore there would be no chance that Harriet
would become pregnant. She quickly rose from the floor and
went to Harriet's bed where she stayed the night with her arms
wrapped lovingly and comforting around her frightened daughter.
Harriet would survive and the scars of this dreadful night would
fade. Her mother's inner strength would be imprinted indelibly
upon Harriet in this moment of terror, rescue and emotional
redemption. No words needed to be spoken as they laid in the
small bed together, each taking comfort from the other.

Chapter 13
Revenge

Several weeks had passed since Jenkins forced himself on Harriet. Once again it was Saturday night and once again, Jenkins was drunk and unconscious. This time he had made it to his bed and had even begun removing his pants, before he slumped back in the bed with his legs dangling from the bed's edge. Hardly a pretty sight, but it could not have been more perfect for what Juliet had been preparing for. Her planned revenge on Jenkins which had first taken hold of her nearly ten years before when Jenkins had thrown Harriet's kitten into a copperhead den, had now become an obsession filled with more hatred for this man than she thought possible of herself.

Jenkins' small two room log cabin with a sleeping loft in the rafters was located 20 feet from the road to Winchester. The low sleeping loft was too hot in the summer and too cold in the winter, so he made his bed in the room off the kitchen. His bed was next to a window so as to better take advantage of a summer night's breeze. Juliet would also use the window to her advantage.

After the assault on Harriet, Juliet had developed her plan more fully and her initial step involved taking a small stick and tying a string to the end of it. At the end of the string she had made a small loop. It looked a bit like a child's homemade fishing pole, but where the hook would normally have been, there was this odd small loop. The easy part of her plan now completed, she now took steps to finalize the plan.

Copperheads were plentiful in wooded rocky areas but one had to be careful catching them. They were highly poisonous. Children had died from their bites and adults had lost fingers when their venom had rotted the flesh.   Choked with fear, Juliet was finally able to capture her deadly prey, and the old feed bag she now carefully carried towards the small log cabin contained 4 of these venomous creatures. As deadly and vile these creatures were, they had a tendency to put off a contradictory sweet smelling scent. This insidious fragrance was often how one knew that a copperhead was close by. Juliet's snake bag had become a bouquet of loathsome and deadly poison. Juliet wanted Jenkins to suffer in the same manner that Harriet's kitten had suffered. Not so much for the sake of the cat, but for the sake of Harriet. Revenge would be served without remorse.

The use of the local copperhead and timber rattler to exact revenge on one's enemy was not as uncommon as one might think. The families that lived in the nearby mountains had been at it for nearly a century, where both the copperhead and timber rattler were plentiful. But, how she would employ her silent and deadly accomplices was undoubtedly more unique than usual. Most settled for the snake to randomly bite their enemy without further direction. Her plan was to choreograph their movements.

She entered stealthily into Jenkins bedroom and untied the sack with the copperheads, laying it carefully between Jenkins legs. She had not fed the snakes since she captured them and they would be hungry and ready to hunt.

Juliet then quietly stationed herself outside by window of Jenkins' bedroom while at the same time retrieving her odd makeshift fishing pole. She could see the snakes beginning to stir in the bag and she needed to work quickly. She dropped the looped string attached to the stick through the window and guided it slowly and carefully over to Jenkins' shriveled manhood. Her heart was pounding which made her task more difficult, but after several tries, she was able to place the loop around around her small target.

The copperheads were agitated and felt the cool air rushing into the bag that held them. The serpents were well aware that an escape route had been provided and they were anxious to find their freedom.......and their next *meal*.

As the copperheads began to slither out of their temporary incarceration, Juliet made short jerking movements on the string. It immediately caught the snakes' attention. Normally a captured snake's first instinct was to flee to safety. Tonight, hunger took precedence. Several noticed movement. For all they knew, it was a mouse and the small rodents were a favorite meal of theirs. Hunger was driving the snakes and two had taken the bait and swiftly struck with fangs angled forward to paralyze their prey with their deadly venom. One of the snakes had, upon striking their prey, taken it into it's gaping mouth. It would be difficult, and in Jenkins' case, nightmarishly painful, to get it to release it's hold.

The resulting screams could be heard all the way to hell and back. A fitting greeting to his future accommodation.

Juliet knew that Jenkins' hands were tied. He couldn't very well point the finger at Juliet without for all practical purposes indicting himself. Even if the attempted rape of Harriet was never mentioned, trying to prove that Juliet had been the culprit would be difficult at best. There would have to be at least a semblance of motivation on Juliet's part to convict her and without the rape mentioned, motivation for the crime would be exhausted. In addition to not being able to show motivation, Bennett Russell and everyone else on this side of the county knew Jenkins had more than a few enemies who would love nothing more than to get even with him for his past misdeeds. He often returned from his Saturday night benders bloodied and bruised from tavern fights and his wounds were hardly the result universal likability.

Juliet felt confident that she would allude all suspicion…...except of course from Jenkins himself. As things stood, Jenkins' very own despicable and vile character had landed him squarely between a rock and a hard place.

For days Jenkins screams and pain induced moaning could be heard from ½ miles away, especially during the dead stillness of the night when sound carried it's furthest. Jenkins laid in his bed with every movement of his body bringing tears to his eyes. The pain was so intense, he rarley slept and when he did, the sleep was brief and full of nightmares about falling in a den of copperheads. He would wake up screaming and soaked in sweat from his hellish dreams, only to realize that the nightmare was more real than not.

Bennett knew there was little one could do about a copperhead bite, but he too had heard Jenkins' blood chilling screams and so he called on a doctor to come out to the farm to see if the doctor could do anything to relieve the poor wretch's agony. He had no affection for this man and believed that whatever he had done to deserve this fate was most likely worthy of such, but still didn't wish this on any man, nor beast. Plus, Bennett needed a good night's rest without his sleep being continually interrupted by the woeful cries of Jenkins.

Dr. Lee entered the squalid cabin of Jenkins and walked to his bedside and pulled up a chair. Bennett had informed him of the location of the bite and he slowly pulled the covers down to expose a blackened mass of large tumor like swellings in the area that had once been his genitals. The sight was so horrific and smell of decaying flesh was so overwhelming, that Dr. Lee, so repulsed by it, turned to vomit on the dirty wooden planks of the floor. He immediately pulled out a handkerchief and placed it over his nose in order to help prevent him from repeating his initial nauseated reaction to Jenkins' .....*injury*.

Dr. Lee got right to the point and said, "Mr. Jenkins. I am sorry to inform you that your wound has turned gangrene. The only chance you have of surviving is to have the infected area amputated, and even then, there is no assurance that the gangrene in your body hasn't already spread to such an extent, that you may very well die regardless of surgery." Truth be known, Dr. Lee had no desire nor stomach to perform a surgery of this nature.

Jenkins had become delirious and from time to time he would grab frantically at his body and throw imaginary copperheads off himself. Dr. Lee saw no reason to continue his visit and left the man a bottle of laudanum, an opium infused elixir, next to his pillow, and then hastily left Jenkins' lair. Chances were, that Jenkins, in the state of mind he was in, would never know that the laudanum was there. Chances were.......Jenkins would not make it through another day.

Chapter 14
Time Moves Slowly On

The summer slid gradually into late fall without any further incident. Jenkins had been buried unceremoniously behind the old log cabin. The Virginia heat and humidity had slowly died behind the colorful Virginia fall foliage and laid to rest in the early winter frost. The trees now stood in skeletal darkness against gray lifeless skies. The activity associated with the court's October term stood in stark contrast to the otherwise lifeless days of winter inactivity. For Juliet, the grains of sand in the hour glass had turned to a thick molasses, taunting her patience. Testing her will.

Bennett Russell had long held a license for a "house of entertainment". It was a general term and with it, one could operate a tavern or one might choose to offer room and board. A place where the weary traveler could get a bite to eat, take a room for the night, or longer, and be able to stable their horse. Bennett had chosen the latter. Taverns invited drunks and fights and he had no desire to be a tavern keeper. His home was located near the corner of the main road to Winchester and a main road to Summit Point and on into Charles Town and so travelers were fairly steady and often in need of a hot meal and bed. Bennett was not one to waste an opportunity to make money. He now owned over 1,500 acres and 20 of his own slaves. There was no doubt that he had become successful, but, as it was with most successful men, the goal line to ultimate success was forever being extended at the work of their own hand.

Although, time in one way seemed to crawl along, the days actually went quickly for Juliet, cooking and cleaning house, not only for Bennett's family, but for all the weary travelers who sought refuge from their journeys. For the next 6 months Juliet lived in an emotional time warp that inexplicably sped up and slowed down with a random will all of it's own.

Chapter 15
The Set Up –Early Fall 1848

After the harvest, Richard Parker held a party at his father's old home, "Soldier's Retreat." It wasn't the most magnificent home in the county, but it certainly stood among the finest. Located at the foot of the Blue Ridge and fronting on the Shenandoah, the soils were as rich as the views themselves. The party was not only for purely social reasons, but also as a way to put his plan into effect. A plan where he would confidentially expose his legal strategy to a *trusted few*, knowing that in such a small community, his plan of misdirection would in short order work it's way back to Philip Williams, the attorney for Bennett Russell.

It was a warm October evening and his 100 or more guests mingled both inside his mansion and outside on the expansive stone balcony overlooking the river. Col. Morgan, who owned over 2,000 acres of prime land several miles west, along with his family attended. Also in attendance were the families of Castleman, Sowers, McCormick, Smith, Lewis, Washington, Ware, Shepherd, and Taliaferro's (the family pronounced their name as Toliver), to just name a few. Enough folks so as to ensure his *false strategy*, would make it's way to Williams, Bennett Russell's attorney.

Throughout the night Parker would play the host, and make small talk with the guest. Inevitably he would be asked about the upcoming trial between Bennett Russell and Juliet. When it came up, he would lean in close to the group that happened to be in his circle at the time, conspiratorially lower his voice, and share a secret that appeared to be meant just for them. He asked them to promise not to say a word about what he was about to say, knowing that it would be all over the county in a matter of days.

The second best thing to a social gathering in itself, was the idle gossip that was shared between neighbors and friends.

Throughout the evening, Parker would reply to their inquiries on the case with, "I shouldn't be saying this" as he theatrically scanned the area for prying eyes and *ears*, "but I trust that this will get no further than just us friends. It has recently come to my attention, that there may be witnesses who claim that the Articles of Agreement had not been signed by the man named Spurr on the date that old man Crafton had purportedly signed, but had done so as much as a week after Crafton had died and therefore, had in essence falsified his witnessing to Mr. Crafton's signature. No doubt, the court would take a very dim view of such shenanigans and therefore would have no alternative but to dismiss the case."

One by one, each group of persons that Parker had quietly assembled assured him that his secret was safe with them. Many would keep this tantalizing story to themselves, but all he needed was one to pass the story on and from there, it would spread at first slowly but then would exponentially gain speed.…... as such juicy gossip has a tendency to do. Parker gave it two weeks before nearly everyone in the county, including Mr. Williams, was aware of his *confidential* conversations.

Parker would find out soon enough if Williams would chase this red herring. Parker had already tried to find the whereabouts of Spurr without any success. With a little luck, Williams would take the bait and spend an inordinate amount of time searching for this Spurr fellow and preparing for a rebuttal of an issue that Parker had no intention of mentioning in court.

Chapter 16
The Trial Continues
October 1848

Finally, the day arrived. The circus was back in town and pedestrians, men on horseback and carriages moved in a steady flow up the hill where the courthouse loomed over all, except for the church which stood like a fortress on the peak of the hill as a reminder of the eternal battle between good and evil. The courthouse as if it were the church's sergeant of arms. Where the church failed in it's constant effort to save the souls of men, the court would then act as the enforcer over the bodies of men. Where one would appeal to man's fear of eternal damnation, the other would appeal to man's earthly fears of being hanged by the neck until dead. Together, they made a formidable team of moral persuasion.

Women were dressed in their Sunday best and protected from the cold weather by bonnet and wool cape. The men were dressed in clothing that protected them from the elements, but the differences in their attire also suggested their station in life. Which rung of the social ladder they stood could not have been more apparent than if they wore a sign around their necks indicating their status or lack thereof.

Juliet once again took her seat in the shadows of the courtroom. All her life she had taken odd jobs for cash which she had put away to eventually purchase her own freedom, but now she used it to pay Parker and if she won, then the money she saved would not only free her, but her entire family. She had in all truth, taken a metaphorical seat at a high stakes card game where it was winner take all.

Sitting in the courtroom were all the witnesses to the Articles of Agreement, save Mr. Spurr. William Spurr could not be found and Williams' nervous habits on this day had uncommonly, followed him into the courthouse. Parker smiled inwardly to himself and realized that Williams had taken the bait and that the absence of Spurr in the courtroom could be used to Parker's own advantage in order to plant more doubt in the juror's minds. Nearly every juror was a slave owner and he would need every advantage possible if he was able to win this trial.

Once again every seat and standing area was filled. The vast majority of people in the courtroom today had heard the *gossip* regarding Spurr. If there was anyone there who hadn't heard this gossip, then they certainly must have just been awakened from a 6 month long sleep. The courtroom was cold and gusts of chilly air would take advantage of the opening doors like an uninvited house cat seeking shelter. Throughout the courtroom there were intermittent vapors of breath that appeared and then disappeared, only to be answered by others throughout the room. A virtual artillery battle of breath, exploding in puffs of vapor. As cold as it was, many were undoubtedly thankful that the typical body odors of summer had been temporarily abated by the frigid air of winter.

Voices rose and fell like competing choirs singing from different hymnals as they excitedly awaited the pompous entrance of the judge that would signal the continuing human drama like the raising of a stage's curtain. Judges seemed to fall in three different categories: the judge that envied the Baptist preacher; the judge who tried to disguise his drinking and envied those whose days of hiding their habit had long since passed; and those who wanted the trial lawyers and other judges to envy them. The current judge barely disguised his affair with old John Barley Corn, but he knew his law and he knew all the tricks of the trade plied by the lawyers who would stand before him. His rather prominent nose had taken on a bluish color over his sixty some years and his face was was blotched with the telltale signs of daily drink. His hair was a coarse gray and fell nearly to his shoulders in the fashion of an era that was quickly fading from memory. If one could judge how long a man had left on this earth by their overall appearance, then certainly, the old judge's time was nearing an end.

As onlookers jockeyed for seats, Juliet, along with most others there that day, noticed a small woman in all black with a bible clutched tightly in her hands like a drowning man clutching desperately at a limb hanging over a swollen river. No doubt that she felt mankind was drowning in a sea of sin. She, for one, planned to keep her head above water.

The woman in black was Anne Page. She was both a religious fanatic and staunch member of the American Colonization Society. The Society opposed slavery, but had in recent years been relegated to the back seat by the Abolitionist movement. The Society, like the abolitionists, worked to end slavery, but unlike the abolitionists, the "Society" held the misguided conviction of not only freeing slaves, but returning them to their home country of Africa. America was the only place that the slaves had ever known and it would be no different than deporting slave *owners* to a country as foreign to them as Africa was to the slaves. But, she had heard the voice of God speaking directly to her, and who was she to question His command. God. The rationalization of the evil of humankind.

Annfield
Home of Anne Page

Juliet couldn't help wondering if this stern looking old woman with the well read bible in her hand, was there hoping that Juliet would be freed, only to have Mrs. Page then attempt to ill conceivably return her to some strange and completely foreign place in Africa known as Liberia.

Mrs. Page had married a wealthy, slave owning planter, with the all important pedigree of Virginia society. Now that Mr. Page had passed on, Mrs. Page was using his accrued wealth to send frightened slaves to what seemed to the slave, the end of the earth. The money she had raised to provide her slaves passage to the dark continent had been earned off the backs of slaves that still worked her plantation. She justified this bizarre irony in the age old belief that God worked in mysterious ways….. and one did not question the word of God. A convenience reserved for the true believer. What Mrs. Page saw as an act of benevolence, was in fact a cruel way to address the sins of slavery.

Anne Page would be remembered by history as little more than a footnote, but an event that had happened at her plantation home in 1807, would have a far greater impact on history in the years to come. On this date, Anne's friend, Mary Custis, who had been visiting Mrs. Page, gave birth to a daughter, she named Mary Anne Randolph Custis. In 1831, Mary Anne Randolph Custis married a young Captain in the Army by the name of Robert E. Lee. In 1861 Lee would reluctantly accept overall command of the Confederate forces who fought to defend the rights of Southerners to own slaves. History seldom moves in a straight line but has twists, turns and overlaps like the limbs on an old hickory tree.

As the judge began to enter the courtroom from a door between the bench and the jury box, a voice loudly proclaimed, "All Rise!"

When the judge settled onto his courtly perch he hammered his hand carved gavel onto the flat of his bench. His gavel had been made for him nearly 20 years ago by an appreciative defendant who had been found innocent by the old judge. The gavel's handle had his name inlaid with a lighter wood and highly stylized. The jarring crack of the gavel was immediately followed with, "This court is now in session for the trial of Bennett Russell and Others vs. Negroes Juliet and Others. Are the counsels prepared to make their argument?"

Philip Williams, counsel for Bennett, quickly stood.

Addressing the judge, he stated, "If it pleases the court, I request that the court postpone this hearing until the next regularly scheduled session of the circuit court."

There was an immediate eruption of disappointment and confusion from those who had prepared for a day of entertainment.

The old judge once again hammered his gavel and sternly countered the audience with, "Order in the court! Order in the court!"

When order had been restored, the judge asked, "And what reason do you have Mr. Williams to request postponement?"

Williams replied, "Unfortunately your honor, one of my key witnesses was unexpectedly unable to attend today's session. His testimony, as to the validity of the Articles of Agreement, is vital to my client and to justice itself."

Judge Douglas replied, "Who is this witness and what reason has he given for not attending my court today?"

Williams could see the not so hidden anger in the judge's eyes and passively replied, "Counsel was unable to locate the whereabouts of Mr. Spurr, a witness to the signing of the Articles of Agreement by Mr. John Russell Crafton."

"Speak up, Mr. Williams!" ordered the judge.

Williams suddenly felt ill and replied, "Your honor, I was unable to find Mr. Spurr."

Laughter broke out and the courtroom and once again the judge demanded order.

Judge Douglas glared at Williams while tapping his finger on his podium. The tapping of a finger seldom struck fear in any man, but today, this simple finger tapping had made Williams' stomach tie in knots.

He then looked over to Parker and asked him if he had any response to Mr. Williams' motion to postpone.

Parker was not going to let Williams off the hook and replied, "Your honor. With all due respect, Mr. Williams has had 6 months in which to arrange for Mr. Spurr's attendance here today. My witnesses have made time in which to respect your honor's own time to this matter, save, one witness of mine. Young Thomas Briggs, who had witnessed the original will in 1839 has recently died. I am afraid that in his present condition, he would be unable to shine any light on the matter here today."

Once again laughter broke out and once again the judge demanded order.

The judge paused for several seconds and then stated, "I tend to agree with Mr. Parker that the plaintiff had more than sufficient time to prepare his witnesses for today's court and that the death of a witness for the defendant could certainly be excused. If your missing witness, Mr. Phillips, had himself died, then your six month search for this mysterious Mr. Spurr would be far more acceptable to this court"

The courtroom erupted in laughter and the judge allowed it to continue longer than was normal as it was he who provoked the laughter. A small perk of being the judge.

Eventually, the judge restored order and then continued, "Therefore, it is the decision of this court that court today will continue and not be postponed. Please proceed Mr. Williams, if indeed you have any further statements relevant to this case."

A somewhat embarrassed Williams assured the judge that he would continue with the examination of the other witnesses to the signing of the Articles of Agreement who were present at court today. One by one, Williams called the witnesses to the signing of the Articles to the witness chair. They included Bennett himself, Bennett's son John, and Bennett's brother Thomas.

Williams had first explained that by law, only 3 witnesses were necessary in validating the signing of a will and therefore, the absence of the fourth witness, Mr. Spurr, was unnecessary and little more than window dressing. Each of William's witnesses swore under oath that the Articles were in fact the wishes of John Russell Crafton and considered the Articles as the last will and testament of Crafton. Williams once again kept it simple for the sake of the jurors and after each witness had testified, he glanced at the jury and then repeated their sworn testimony as it would best relate to his client.

When Williams completed his examination of the witnesses, the judge stated, "Your witnesses, Mr. Parker."

Parker stood, and before calling the first witness for cross examining stated, "So Mr Spurr could not be found. Certainly convenient for the plaintiff."

This immediately brought an objection by Williams and the judge directed the jury to ignore the statement by Parker and then scolded Parker for what the judge called a cheap tactic that had no place in his court. Parker knew he would be reprimanded by the judge, but it was too late to do any good. Another seed had been planted in the jury's mind.

Order restored, Parker then called for Bennett Russell to take the stand.

Parker rested his hand on the railing of the witness chair's berth and gently tapped his fingers for several seconds before directing his line of questioning to Bennett.

Parker asked that Bennett to state his name and then proceeded with, "It is typical...no, let me rephrase that. It is without question that the witnessing of a will is *never* witnessed by those who have an interest in the estate of the man writing his will. This is done for obvious purposes so as to not give the sinister appearance that the dying man had been in any way been coerced by the those who might benefit. So my question to you, Mr. Russell, is that do you in anyway benefit from your father's will?"

Bennett answered, "Mr. Crafton was my father and he intended to leave his children his estate as is customary with a father and his children." Bennett attempted to add more to his statement but was cut off by Parker, stating that he had answered the question and nothing more needed to be added.

Parker continued, "Then the answer, as I understand you, is *yes*. You stood to benefit from your father's will and against all convention, you decided to witness his will even though you had many nearby neighbors as well as a constant flow of travelers to your home that had no connection to Mr. Crafton! There are no further questions, Mr. Russell. You may now step down."

Parker then asked the same questions of the other two witnesses of the Articles which resulted in the same answers. The cultivation of more seeds of doubt within the jury's minds.

Next, Parker called Thomas Briggs, followed by his son Pitt, to the witness stand.

"Mr. Briggs, I would like to first say how sorry I was to hear about the sudden death of your son, Thomas, Jr.. He will be missed by our entire community and it is a tribute to you, that he will remain in the minds of all of us here today for many years to come."

Parker then shifted into his role of defense attorney and asked, "How long had you known Mr. Crafton?"

Briggs answered, "My family has known Mr. Crafton from nearly the time that my father started his import/export business in Stafford County. Mr. Crafton's father, Bennett Crafton, also owned an import/export business a little further south in King William County. Being engaged in the same business, their paths would often cross and over time, my father and Bennett Crafton became friends. Bennett Crafton was also a surveyor and read law. One of my brothers became a surveyor and another became an attorney. No doubt from the influence of Mr. Crafton had on our early lives. When Bennett Crafton left Virginia in 1776 to join the army in Granville, NC., John Russell Crafton was a small child and was left with his mother to raise on her own. Major Bennett Crafton spent the next 7 years in the army and died in South Carolina in 1785 while on a business trip. John was left orphaned when his mother died during latter part of the war. Sadly, no money was forthcoming to properly care for him. My father did what he could for John and offered him a job in his own import/export business to help transport goods from the coast to points inland. When John Russell Crafton became an adult, he struck out on his own as a teamster in his own business."

Parker continued, "Would you say that Mr. Crafton trusted you and your family?"

"He did." responded Briggs.

"Was it Mr. Crafton's intention to free his slaves upon his own death?" inquired Parker.

"It was his intention, sir." Briggs replied.

Parker then asked, "Were you surprised when you heard that a second will was presented by Mr. Crafton's heirs directing that the heirs sell the slaves upon his death? If indeed you were surprised, could you please elaborate."

Briggs paused in thought before answering, "I, for one, was quite surprised. Mr. Crafton had on a number of occasions expressed his desire to free his slaves. The will that myself and my two sons had witnessed was the final culmination of his desire. He knew that he would need to hire out the slaves during his fading time on this earth in order to provide for his basic needs, but at no time did he ever suggest that the slaves should be sold in order to do so. Certainly, the hiring out of the slaves should have covered his financial needs and sale of the slaves upon his death would hardly have been necessary in order to accomplish his financial needs."

"Objection, your honor!" Williams proclaimed. "Mr. Briggs could not know what was in the mind of Mr. Crafton 3 years later in 1842 when the Articles were signed by Mr. Crafton. Circumstances change, and it is apparent that circumstances had changed when Mr. Crafton suffered a stroke. I ask the court to strike this last statement by Mr. Briggs."

"Objection sustained. Strike from the record only that portion where Mr. Briggs speculated that the sale of the slaves would not have been necessary to provide for Mr. Crafton's financial needs. There would be no way for Mr. Briggs to have been privy to the actual costs of Mr. Crafton's care or the income that may have resulted from the hiring out of the slaves in question." ruled the judge.

Parker had no desire to challenge the objection. Although, Briggs has stated what was most likely the truth, his statement could only be proven if records had been kept in regard to the cost of Mr. Crafton's care and there were no records that he was aware of. If the jury illogically assumed that the costs of Mr. Crafton's care actually exceeded the revenue from hiring out the slaves, then it would indicate that Crafton's physical condition was so extensive that he may not have been capable of physically signing the Articles. Also, if his physical condition was the result of a stroke, then it would logically follow that soundness of mind would be questionable. Parker felt that the plaintiff's attorney would have great difficulty attempting to prove one without leaving an opening for the other. Parker was ready to lay the trap.

"One last question, Mr. Briggs. Had you seen Mr. Crafton after he had suffered his stoke and prior to the alleged signing by him of the said Articles of Agreement? And furthermore, what was his condition at that time?"

Briggs responded, "To the best of my memory, I had stopped by to see Mr. Crafton when I had heard he suffered a stroke, which I believe to have been quite near the time that the Articles of Agreement were shortly thereafter signed. Mr. Crafton was unresponsive and had suffered paralysis as a result of the stroke."

Parker then asked Briggs, "Was Mr. Crafton able to utilize his extremities such as being able to walk, or to feed himself or have the ability to hold anything in his hand without the aid of others?"

Briggs replied to the question, "I was saddened to see Mr. Crafton in this condition. I took his hand in mine, but his hand seemed lifeless and incapable of using such."

"I have no further questions, your honor", Parker concluded.

The judge then said, "Your witness, Mr. Williams."

Williams stood and approached the witness. "Are you a doctor, Mr Briggs?"

Briggs answered no and Williams continued, "So, you are not a doctor, yet you brazenly make medical diagnoses without any training whatsoever in the field of medicine."

Williams left his cross examination there for the time being and stated to the court, "I have no further questions."

Parker then called Mr. Briggs' son Pitt to the stand and basically followed the same line of questioning that he had done so with his father, Thomas Briggs. Same objections and same results. Parker knew that most of the jurors had at some time in their life seen family or friends who had suffered a stroke and suspected that the jury fully understood the debilitating consequences of a stroke. It does not take a doctor to tell most people what is clearly obvious. Although a portion of the Briggs family testimony had been stricken from the record, it was not so easy to strike it from the minds of the jurors.

Neither attorney was ready for closing arguments and there was still the question of the mysterious fourth witness to the signing of the Articles. The questionable Mr. Spurr. Williams had spent much of his time preparing for a stringent examination of a witnesses who claimed that Spurr had actually signed the Articles well after the death of Crafton and therefore had committed fraud. When Parker had not called witnesses to the stand to that effect, he smelled a rat, but without Spurr in court today, Williams could not altogether discount the rumor he had heard. Parker could very well be holding this witness of his in reserve for a coup de grace. He was also well aware that Parker had effectively cast dispersion and suspicion on his client and would need to provide character witnesses to testify on behalf of his clients. Instead of a defendant having to defend their position, the plaintiffs had effectively been put on the defensive.

The judge now spoke, "Before this court is adjourned, it is ordered that the slaves involved in this suit be removed from the plaintiff's farm to be hired out indefinitely until this case is resolved. The purpose of removing the slaves from their natural home is for the slave's own benefit. In similar cases, much mischief has been practiced by the slave owners that had resulted in the slave's punishment and even the illicit sale of the slaves prior to the conclusion of manumission case in question. It is therefore ordered that the plaintiffs find suitable employment for the said slaves within 30 days and keep a strict accounting of Mr. Crafton's estate. I hereby order Mr Bennett Russell to act as administrator of John Russell Crafton's estate and to provide copies of the accounting to this court. This court is hereby continued until the next regularly scheduled hearing in May 1849."

Juliet sat frozen in her chair. The judges order was to her, the equivalent of a northeaster winter storm, paralyzing everything in it's path. In all likelihood, her family would not be hired out to just one person. It was rare that someone would hire all 14 of her family. Her family would almost certainly be split up. She had not considered this a possibility and now, that which had initially frozen her solid, began to melt into tears. The nightmare of all slaves was the possibility of family separation and now that nightmare had given way to harsh reality. What was once like an unseen demon in the darkness had now come alive and burst through the door of consciousness, ripping her heart out in the process.

Chapter 17
A Family Divided

As Juliet sat motionless on the back of the wagon, the heavens themselves seemed to weep, as a steady rain fell that not so much washed away her tears, but rather, hid them. The stain of her tears could never be washed away. They would instead, mark forever, her heart. An inner pain that acted as a preview of what was to come if she did not win her and her family's freedom.

Moses found Juliet puddled upon the dirt floor of their quarters within the summer kitchen. No sound was coming from her. No movement. Barely a breath. Moses thought her dead and rushed to her, taking her lifeless form in his arms. To his relief, her eyes opened as she lifted her hand gently to his cheek. She knew he would not fully understand the tragedy about to unfold. Looking into Moses' eyes she saw his innocent pleading and her river of emotion burst loose, not so much for herself, but for sweet and innocent Moses who needed Juliet. Relied on Juliet. And loved her unquestionably. Juliet did not know how Moses would survive. Her body heaved with more force than ever before and Moses did not ask her why, but gently rocked her in his strong arms. His God given sweetness and goodness only served to constrict further her chest, throat and heart. The only sound she now made was like the soft whimper of a little girl waking up from a bad dream.

Chapter 18
A New Approach

As the courtroom cleared on that brisk October day in 1848, Williams asked Bennett to stop by his office before returning home. The events of the day had shaken his confidence in regard to any outright win for his client and he was already preparing to implement a strategy that could ensure ultimate victory.

Bennett Russell was delayed leaving the courthouse grounds by well wishers and now, even the press had taken interest in the case. If they hoped to get anything more from Bennett than what they had already knew, they were sadly mistaken. Bennett thanked them all for attending today's trial but said little more.

Thirty minutes later, Bennett opened the door to Williams' office and said, "Philip. You wanted to see me."

Williams gestured to a chair and said, "Please, take a seat Bennett." Once Bennett had taken the seat offered, Williams continued. "I am sure you are aware of Mr. Parker's legal defense strategy of placing doubt in the juror's minds regarding the legality of the Articles of Agreement."

Bennett shifted uncomfortably in his chair and merely said, "I am and I doubt you brought me here to state the obvious. Please get on with it."

Russell's motionless stare was unsettling for Williams, but he nevertheless continued, "This trial may go on for longer than either one of us one have predicted. I have concerns about putting the outcome of the trial in the juror's hands. At least at this time. It is my opinion that the trial, at best, would end in a hung jury and that would not bode well for a retrial. What I have in mind is to employ delaying tactics in order to avoid a jury that is currently sitting on a fence and not knowing which side they will fall."

Bennett Russell promptly spoke up, "So. Your idea, Philip, is for me to spend more money so as to pay you to represent me indefinitely?   A plan that benefits you personally, I would say."

Williams calmly replied, "Not indefinitely, Bennett, but long enough to financially break Juliet. Her funds are quite limited. To what extent exactly, I can't say, but her funds do not compare with your own funds. Without the funds to pay an attorney, Juliet will be left defenseless and that is when we will attack and get the last word in at our closing argument. Yes. I know what you are thinking and you will have to spend more money, but far more money will be made on the sale of the slaves that will more than offset any costs to yourself."

Bennett sat still, considering this legal approach. It was not unheard of for attorneys to drag things out, especially in suits of manumission. Frustration, lack of funding and even death, had handed both plaintiffs and defendants the a desired ruling by the courts. It was more like the strategy of attrition. Starve those in the fortress and they will eventually surrender. It was no doubt in Bennett's mind that he certainly held the advantage.

The silence in the office, which to Williams seemed far longer than was in reality, was finally broken with Bennett replying, "So be it."

Before Bennett got to the door to leave Williams stated, "One other thing, Bennett. I do not want Spurr to testify in court and be open to cross examination by Parker. I will try to persuade the court to allow him to sign a paper in front of another attorney and witnesses, wherever he may be at that time, stating that he had indeed witnessed the signing of the Articles of Agreement by your father as well as state that your father was of sound mind when doing so. I believe I can get the court to agree to this request."

Bennett said nothing, but thought to himself that Spurr may very well had things in his past that would best be left in the past. Not having him in court would help assure such. Attacking a man's character without him present to defend himself could easily be shown as nothing more than a cheap ploy by the attorney who was desperate and was resorting to slanderous behavior. Letting sleeping dogs lie has more than once kept one from being bitten.

Bennett made a small nod of his head, made his exit and disappeared down the street.

Williams let out a long and much relieved breath. He had not been sure how Bennett would react to his proposed strategy, but now that they were on the same page, his nervous tics subsided.

Chapter 19
Court Day Again
May 1849

Juliet sat at her familiar chair hidden in the partial darkness of the courtroom with her head bowed. She held her hands together in front of her, slowly rubbing them together. She had little feeling in her hands after a winter of gathering stones from the fields and loading them into a wagon to be used to build stone walls on her temporary *masters* farm.

Life was more harsh at the farm she had been hired out to. Her life had never been easy, but the back breaking work of loading stone 10 hours a day made the old days seem glorious in comparison. Her hands were cracked and weathered like a woman twice her age. The palms of her hands had become so toughened by callouses, that by spring she could literally grab the handle of an iron skillet off the fire with her bare hands without pain or injury. During those winter days, toes were often frozen and some blackened, only to be removed and then the toe-less creatures would be sent back to these hellish fields of rock the very next day. During days of freezing rain, men's beards would inhumanely sparkle with a thick coating of ice.

After each day of loading stone, Juliet would then pray each night for snowstorms to bury that never ending supply of rocks. On those snowy days where nothing moved, she found brief respite from what many called "rock cropping." Rocks were the crop of winter. They even seemed to grow right out the ground where just a year before, other rocks had lain and been carried away, or thrown in large piles to be retrieved at a later time. Men had for years thrown themselves against the rock in this part of the world only to see themselves broken and defeated. But, it never stopped them. Not as long as they had slaves.

As court settled in and the judge took his seat at the bench, he gave a directive that stunned the courtroom. Judge Douglas had just demanded that the attorneys give closing arguments. Neither attorney was prepared for closing arguments and exchanged looks of surprise and confusion. The judge was old and had his occasional bouts with general wellness that was to be expected of a man his age. What hadn't been expected were the little signs of confusion that followed these illnesses. Nevertheless, he was the judge and whatever the judge ruled was to be obeyed.

Both attorneys had to rely on their previous arguments and stumble through a closing argument they were wholly unprepared to give. Once closing arguments were given by the attorneys for the plaintiff and the defendant, the judge directed the jury to make their decision and were led out of the jury box to a small room located just off the courtroom. Both attorneys quickly huddled with their clients attempting to explain that which they themselves could not understand.

The jury disappeared behind closed doors at 10:00 in the morning. Juliet sat motionless, frozen within the reality of the moment. The court room was finally cleared of the public who had attended today's session but no one who had attended that day left for their homes, but found refuge at taverns, or if they were lucky, at the home of a friend who lived in town. They would patiently wait for word that the jury had returned.

Nearly seven hours later the jury returned. The word spread throughout the town and a mad dash was made for the courthouse.

The jury sat nervously in their assigned seats in the jury box and waited as the crowds noisily found their own seats. When the judge was satisfied that court could be reconvened and brought to order he once again hammered his gavel and said, "Have the gentleman of the jury come to a decision?"

The jury's foreman awkwardly stood as if seeking shelter from unknown forces. With reddened face he made his announcement. Juliet closed her eyes. The foreman stated, "Your honor, the jury…...the jury was unable to agree on a decision."

Most persons attending court were not sure what this non-decision meant. Did Juliet win her freedom by some type of legal reasoning, or had she lost her quest for freedom? People turned to others beside them, in back of them and in front of them with all of them talking at once seeking an answer to their confusion. What began as murmurs turned into full out shouting.

It took the judge nearly 5 minutes to restore order in the court. His voice became hoarse and he pounded the gavel like an insane carpenter who could not strike the nail. With order finally restored he spoke. "Although I had hoped that the jury would have been able to make a decision, it is apparent that a decision could not be reached. If the attorney for the plaintiff does not request a retrial, then the will recorded by the defendants known as Negroes Juliet and Others, shall be considered the last will and testament of John Russell Crafton and the defendants shall be freed as so directed in such will of John Russell Crafton."

Juliet held her breath and made a silent prayer that her days as a slave had come to an end.

The judge continued, "But, if the plaintiff chooses to go forward with their case they shall make their desire known today by requesting a retrial and submitting the proper legally written request to this court within 2 weeks of this date. If indeed a retrial is to occur, a new jury will be selected at the October session of court. How say thee Mr. Williams?

Williams looked back at his client and Bennett Russell nodded his head. Williams then stood and answered Judge Douglas. "Your honor, my client wishes to request a retrial and I shall have all the proper paperwork and any court fees that may be required or have been incurred from today's court within the two week period so directed by his honor."

With one swift movement, the judge struck his gavel and stated, "Gentlemen of the jury, the court thanks you for your service and you are hereby dismissed. The next session of court will be held in October of this year. Court is now adjourned."

Juliet looked pleadingly at Parker and her eyes told him everything. He had to explain that it would all begin over again as if the past year had never happened. He would have rather walked through fire, but he unfortunately did not have that option. As Parker explained this to Juliet, her body slumped so dramatically that her clothing appeared to no longer hold a body within it.

In October of 1849 both attorneys gathered in court to go through the process of selecting a new jury. In May of 1850, the judge once again, appearing irritated and anxious to get this case over with one way or the other, ordered the jury to be sequestered and to render a decision. Once again, the jury could not make a decision. And still again, the same orders were read by the judge and again, the plaintiff requested a retrial. And again, Juliet rode away in the back of the wagon, leaving another part of her soul behind to haunt the courthouse for an eternity.

Chapter 20
The Death of Judge Douglas and the Ascent of Parker

The strategy of delay by Williams was now in full effect. He had gotten the court to agree to Spurr's long distance testimony using a variety of arcane legal maneuvers to postpone court, but nothing could have been more unexpected and devastating to Juliet's case than the death of Judge Douglas and the subsequent election of Richard Parker to the 13th circuit court of Virginia in the latter part of 1851. As a duly elected judge to the very court in which he represented Juliet, Parker would no longer be able to represent her, nor could the trial be held in Clarke County with Parker sitting on the bench. The trial was therefore moved to neighboring Frederick County, which resulted in more delays.

Williams could barely believe his good luck. Not only had Parker's election created a postponement of the trial that he himself did not have to request under some additional flimsy excuse, a new jury would have to be selected. A new jury selection meant more delays and more importantly, that the seeds of doubt, carefully planted in the former jury's mind by Parker, would no longer be as much of an issue for Williams. Certainly, the new jury would be briefed on previous testimony, but it would not have the same impact on them. Lastly, Parker had been a clever and effective counsel for Juliet and the chance that he could be replaced with an equally astute attorney was improbable. Williams was indeed pleased with the turn of events. Pleased, indeed!

———————————————————————

Bennett reflected for a moment on the news of Parker's election and what this would mean to his chances of emerging as the victor. He didn't need Williams to explain the obvious. What wasn't as obvious to either of the attorneys was the primary motivation behind Bennett's determination to have the Articles of Agreement be recorded as the last will and testament of his father. Bennett had, through hard work and calculated risks, become the most successful of all his siblings. With his success, came responsibilities to his family. Not just his wife and children, but to his brothers and sisters. His brother Thomas, had not been lucky and his second business venture had just gone under. John and his family were preparing to move west and start a new life rife with risks not yet even considered. James had not been able to secure a loan for his own land to farm and Bennett had, for all practical purposes, given him 300 acres to farm and create a secure life for his own family. His three sisters had married good men but not men with a great deal of means. Each of his siblings looked upon Bennett to help provide for them as he was able and willing, but, at the same time they never demanded of him nor were they jealous of him. His father had little to leave each of them, other than the slaves, and the sale of the slaves would help give each one of his siblings a chance at a better life. Bennett could be ruthless in business, but behind his success driven toughness was a man where family came first. Bennett and his siblings had always been there for one another while growing up and as the oldest, they had all looked to Bennett when their father was gone on business trips delivering goods, which was more often than not. Bennett did not need the money from the receipts of the slave's auction. He was well off and his share of the money from the sale of the slaves would have little impact on his own life, but the share his siblings would receive would be a blessing in disguise. If not for Bennett's siblings, Juliet and her family would have their freedom but his obligation to family came first. At the expense of Juliet's own family.

Chapter 21
Murder

 Even the most hardened slave owner was shocked when the news reached them. The anti-slavery forces were outraged and were calling for the end of slavery immediately…..and for good reason. Col. James Castleman and his son Stephen had been charged in the murder of one of their own slaves.

 The *exact* cause of the slave Lewis's death was the typical speculation that surrounded most murder cases, but what was not being challenged was that Col. Castleman had accused Lewis of theft and had inhumanely and with monstrous intent flogged him so severely that his back was purported to have been a sickening fleshless picture of raw meat and bone. What was in dispute was whether the Castleman's, after the beating had hanged Lewis or had Lewis, in such pain and agony, hanged himself. Most the Castleman's neighbors in Clarke County, even though they may not have said, believed that Castleman, in a fit of mindless fury, hanged poor Lewis for no other reason than he had not immediately died from a beating that any normal man would not have survived.

 Richard E. Parker, Juliet's former attorney, was now Judge Parker, serving both Clarke and Jefferson Counties and would normally had presided over the trial Col. Castleman and his son at the October term of court was replaced by request of Castleman stating that because of Parker's representation for the past 3 years of Juliet in her fight for freedom, would not be able to receive a fair trial. Judge Samuels of Shenandoah County was appointed to preside over the murder trial of Lewis.
 Bennett Russell's attorney, Phillip Williams, who had just

recently been feeling more confident in his case against Juliet, now was unsure. The hideous murder of the slave Lewis would hang in the air for years and he felt that if a jury in Bennett's and Juliet's trial met to determine the outcome of their case too soon after the trial of Castleman, a residual compassion for Juliet could exist and thus change the outcome in favor of Juliet. It was more important than ever that Williams used every legal or not so legal tactic to stall and postpone the trial initiated by his client, Bennett. It was imperative that the senseless and insanely cruel act by Castleman be allowed to fade from the minds of the general public, if indeed this murderous act would fade, but his options were limited. Williams would postpone court for as long as he possibly could.

The news and the description of Lewis' death wasn't limited to just the white people in the area, but to every slave as well. The revulsion and fear that these enslaved people felt ran the gamut from rebellion, and escape to trembling submission.

For Juliet, she no longer had Parker to be her rock of strength and calm. He had been elected judge and see remained in limbo not only without Parker, but without any attorney whatsoever. The possibility of freedom now seemed a distant and quickly retreating dream. At no point in the past 3 years had she felt so close to giving up….but her natural fortitude of character would not let her be submissively defeated. She had entered this fight and she would finish it, regardless of the outcome.

_____

Col. Castleman was a prominent citizen of the county and it undoubtedly played a major part in the court's decision. After 2 days of court at the October session, Castleman was found not guilty of murder. There were few cheers for him personally, but there was a mixed feeling of relief for others who owned slaves. The verdict had assured them that they still had control of the law and their own destiny as superiors.

It was later found that Lewis had not been the thief. Castleman apologized for his mistake. Hell always had room for one more. It wasn't long before the newspapers throughout the northern states reported on this atrocity and the abolitionist were quick to fan the flames. Word had it that some well known woman abolitionist by the name of Stowe was in the process of writing a book based in part on this very same case. A reckoning was soon to come.

Chapter 22
Juliet Gets a New Attorney

In addition to the upsetting news of having to find a new attorney, Juliet's family had been hired out to various local farmers and businessmen in need of temporary help. Sundays were the only time that Juliet and her family could potentially see one another, and then, only those who were within walking distance. Juliet's spirit, as well as her meager savings, continued to dwindle as the trial continued. A sense of desperation took hold of all of Juliet's family. What could possibly be worse than being a slave, was to be a slave with the prospect of freedom, and then seeing the sweetness of hope slowly dissolve into the real and bitter prospect of defeat.

Parker had come to talk to Juliet after his election to explain why he could no longer represent her. Whether either one of them admitted it, a bond had developed between them. They were two very different people from two very different worlds, but it was natural that after 3 years that they would become more than the typical relationship between client and attorney. The respect they had for one another did not need to be fawning, or even spoken in the most basic of ways. True respect comes from *acta non verba,* actions, not words. For Parker, who would no longer be able to represent Juliet, he was torn with conflicting emotions of having been elected a judge and those feelings of guilt for abandoning Juliet. Although he had wanted this judgeship, he would not have been terribly disappointed had he not won, especially now, as he stood before Juliet. The words that normally came so naturally to him, suddenly seemed trite and inappropriate. As he spoke, his words were punctuated with awkward extended periods of silence, but it was the silence that spoke far more than his words. It was during these silent moments that the language of the heart could be heard.

Robert Young Conrad

   The attorney that Parker had recommended to replace him was named Robert Y. Conrad, a successful lawyer in Winchester. Parker had not only settled on recommending Conrad to Juliet because of his legal acumen, but also for his connections to the legal community in Winchester and Frederick County. The trial's venue was ordered to be moved to Frederick County and having a familiar and respected face before the court and judge of that locality certainly would not hurt and hopefully would be beneficial to Juliet's freedom quest.

Robert Conrad was in his mid 40s and at the very peak of his legal acumen. Conrad had at first decided on a career in the military and had attended the United States Military Academy before leaving for a career in law. Conrad was a serious man, a patient man, but also a bullheaded man. The latter trait both was both a strength and a weakness. Time would tell if this trait would benefit or hurt Juliet's case. Parker had gambled that Conrad's single minded determination would benefit Juliet.

Conrad had married into the powerful and wealthy Powell family of Loudoun County which helped raise his own stature in the community, although it also brought about the stress of living up to the ideals of the southern gentrified society. Betty Powell Conrad, like so many young women who had been raised in luxury, was better suited to the gaiety of balls than the responsibilities of being a wife. Making the transition from a care free life of a privileged young woman to the tedious and boring duties of marriage was made even more difficult by Conrad's extended travels away from her. As with all ambitious men, paving the way to higher success, both socially and career wise, had to be obtained wherever that path may lead, and often the path was distant and lonely. His absence from a wife, who expected to be the primary focus in his life, would lead to petty arguments. But, the one thing that was certain was that they loved one another deeply, and therefore would always resolve any of their differences.

Conrad was a hard worker, but one who used brain over brawn

and therefore, like most men his age and in his position, his face betrayed a fleshy softness. He was fastidious about his dress and appearance, never appearing in public in less than impeccability. Slavery was a way of life for most Southerners and Conrad was no different. As a man of law and not of plantations, he himself needed only house servants and not the number of slaves that others in the planter order would require. Therefore, slavery to him was more genteel in nature and did not have the harshness otherwise reserved for the field hands of plantation owners. He had no direct understanding of slavery's true world, that was in many ways foreign to him.

Despite the nature of the case he was about to handle and his more refined urban ways that potentially could hamper his insight to the case, the one thing Conrad did have, was an overwhelmingly competitive nature.

Regardless of his physically soft appearance, he could be as tough as an old oak tar bucket. He looked forward to testing his mettle against the establishment and had already poured over Parker's notes and court proceedings, readying himself for battle. His time at West Point had certainly influenced the way he saw law. Plan for the enemies strategy and tactics, build your own strategy and tactics based on your knowledge of the enemy, attack with precision and never retreat. Always make your enemy react to your own offensive and use a defensive stance only when necessary.

Of course, a single mindedness approach to any battle, militarily or not, had it's weaknesses and a good field commander could always exploit a single mindedness approach.

Robert Y. Conrad Home
Winchester, Virginia

Chapter 23
A Run to Freedom

Juliet's son Marshall was now 15 years old and bigger than most men twice his age. In this regard, Marshall took after his father. His pride had come from his mother, although, young men at this age had neither the patience or wisdom, that can only come with time, could temper the pride. He was neither a man, nor a boy, but like young men this age, they still had a strong attachment to their mothers, whether they admitted it or not. When sick, injured or afraid, they would turn to their mother and the youthful cockiness of a boy flirting with manhood, would vanish, leaving in it's place the little boy that had for awhile, been kidnapped by the relentless specter of adulthood.

Robert Briggs, another son of Thomas Briggs, had hired Juliet for a one year period. He was a man who knew that small children could not be split up from their mother and had therefore taken up the care of four of Juliet's youngest. Marshall would not be one of those who remained with Juliet and because of the distance between the Briggs farm and the farm that Marshall had been hired out to, he was not able to visit her and his younger siblings on Sundays. Week after week, the hole in Marshall's heart seemed to widen. He would vacillate between anger and despondency. His patience with the continued trial was unraveling as well.

Marshall had decided to take matters in his own hands and run for freedom, but he was unsure as to his escape route. His emotions would in the end, guide him. Directing him to the one thing that freedom could not replace.

Marshall waited until the moon had faded away where darkness would hide his clandestine movements. He knew where his first leg of the journey would take him, but beyond that, he didn't know. He would play it by ear and hope for the best.

———————————————

Sheriff Isler rode into Peter Cain's farm mid morning, one day after the full moon had vanished into darkness and 2 days before it's resurrection.

Cain had been expecting the Sheriff and was near his house doing chores so that he wouldn't miss the Sheriff's arrival.

Isler called out, "Peter! What can you tell me about the disappearance of Marshall?"

Cain owned a small farm on Senseny Road. He fancied himself a self appointed preacher of the gospel and had constructed a small flimsily framed building on his property that became known as "Cain's Chapel." It barely seated 20 persons, although, there was never a fear of ever overcrowding.

Cain had never learned to read but had partially memorized biblical passages from his years of listening to sermons. The rest he just made up as he went along with non-existent passages such as angels riding fire breathing dragons smiting and smoting as they went. Since his normal 3-5 person congregation were also illiterate, his rather fantastical sermons were accepted without question.

Cain replied to the Sheriff, "I had taken out Marshall's dinner last night around sunset and then came in to have my own dinner and then went straight to bed. That was the last I saw of him."

Sheriff Isler looked into the distance as if he would catch sight of Marshall, and then said, "He's on foot and if he could cover a mile in approximately a half hour period of time, so he could be a far as 20 miles away, but only if he didn't take breaks and chances are, when dawn came he would hunker down somewhere so as to not be seen. I'm guessing that he could not be further than 10 miles away and I will put out the word that there is a runaway slave and for everyone in the area to keep an eye out for any black man by himself walking any of the roads or fields."

Cain then said, "I ain't paying Mr. Russell for the use of his boy! He left me high and dry and if I can't get in my crop, Russell is gonna have to pay me for my losses!"

Isler sighed and said, "That would be between you and Bennett, Cain."

Isler then mounted his horse and looked over to Cain and said, "Have a good day, Peter."

Peter Cain then replied, "Have a good day, my ass!"

Isler rode off and could hear Cain preaching some made up scripture full of fire and brimstone. Isler was relieved that he wasn't there to be Cain's personal congregation as he rode past Cain's makeshift chapel.

Isler returned to his office in Berryville and it wasn't long before Robert Briggs rode in with Marshall in tow. It would seem that Marshall, cold, hungry and afraid had walked the 5 miles to Robert's farm where Juliet had been hired out.

Marshall remained quiet throughout the wagon ride from town to Bennett's farm. Marshall's eyes betrayed alternate fear and anger. Marshall was larger and more muscled than Isler. He certainly would have had no problem overpowering Isler should he decide to do so. Isler had decided to take no chances and had cobbled Marshall's legs and tied his hands behind his back.

Isler pulled his wagon into Bennett's lane to his house and could see Bennett standing on the porch with his 3 beloved hounds. He had already heard from a local man who was on his way to Winchester that Marshall had run away. News of this nature always traveled fast.

Isler stepped down from his rickety wagon leaving a sullen Marshall sitting in the back leaning against the sideboards and said, "Good morning, Bennett. Your boy is in the wagon. What do you want me to do with him?"

Bennett knew that Cain would be upset about having paid for Marshall's services that would now not be fulfilled. He would deal with Cain later. Bennett had more pressing matters he wanted addressed and asked, "Why did Marshall run? Had he been mistreated?"

Isler responded, "Not that I can see, Bennett. He has a number of scratches on his arms, legs and face, but I suspect that was from the brambles he passed through while escaping."

Bennett then asked, "Then, what reason would you suspect that

Marshall ran, other than running is always in the back of every slave's mind?"

The Sheriff shifted from one leg to the other and said, "You're right about slaves always dreaming of running to freedom, but..." Isler hesitated for a moment.... "Mr. Briggs said that he found Marshall sleeping on the floor of Juliet's slave quarters..... with his head in his mother's lap this morning. It would seem that Marshall just plain missed his mother."

Bennett thought back for a moment. He had watched slave auctions where families were sold off to different masters, and had heard the wailing of those poor wretches as they were led away from their family, never to see them again. Even young calves that were being weaned from their mothers, bawled for several day before settling down. Bonds between mothers and their offspring were strong, no matter whether it be animal or human. Bennett did not believe in physically punishing a slave. The effect of corporeal punishment was at best short term and too often lead to more serious problems down the road. There were better ways to get one's desired results and Isler had unknowingly just provided that avenue for Bennett.

Bennett instructed Isler to remove Marshall's chains and to return to town, but not before Isler informed Bennett Russell that he would have to pay a $5 jail fee. Fines and penalties were how Isler made his salary and he was hardly going to let it be forgotten. Bennett paid without question. It was to be expected. Marshall would be worth at least $1200 at auction and $5 was a good investment.

When Marshall walked up to Bennett, his eyes were cast downward. Bennett let him stand that way for a full minute before saying, "Marshall. You will not be whipped, beaten or chained."

Marshall then looked up with both surprise and wariness.

Bennett continued, "Understand this, Marshall. If you run again, I will not hesitate to hire out Juliet as far south as possible and to the most cruel man that I can find. Do you understand me, Marshall?"

Marshall's entire body seemed to sag and his eyes told Bennett everything he needed to know.

Marshall would do nothing to jeopardize his mother's well being. He had not expected this and hated Bennett Russell more than if he had been given 50 lashes of the whip. But, he knew he had been bested, and had no choice other than to submit.

Marshall answered Bennett with the only answer he could possibly give which was, "Yes suh."

Bennett then finished up with, "I will make other arrangements for your hiring out and in the meantime, take the slave quarters closest to the house." Bennett would deal with Cain and the hiring out of Marshall later in the day.

Marshall walked dejectedly and slowly back to the quarters he had been told to go with even a greater feeling of helplessness than he had had just 2 days before. His face had been covered with dust from the wagon ride, save a single slender trail that had been washed by a single tear.

Chapter 24
Taking It's Toll
1853 to 1854

It had been 5 years since Juliet first began the defense of her freedom, but her face was beginning to show the physical and emotional toll of uncertainty and harsh labor. The effect on her was not limited to the external appearance but was also had battered her very soul. Her once proud and near flawless face was now weathered with the premature aging of toil and worry. Lines that had begun at the corner of her eyes had deepened and lengthened down her face. She had not yet turned 40 years old but she appeared to be a woman many years older. Her soul was beginning to unravel from the constant emotional stress of the trial and only from her sheer power of will had she kept it from becoming a tattered and empty inner shell that had once been full of grace, strength and a shinning light that shone on all of those she loved.

On a day after she had been hired out to the McCormick family, she noticed a reflection coming from a small sinkhole on the property that the McCormick family used to dispose of their broken china, useless farm equipment parts and carcasses of sheep and cattle that had been found in the fields and no longer fit for human consumption. Juliet curiously approached the old sinkhole and discovered that the reflection coming from the pit were pieces of an old looking glass. She reached down and took out the largest sliver of glass from the broken remains and lifted it up to her face. A tightness developed in her chest as she saw the reflection of a woman she barely knew. She began to angle the glass with the hope that the reflection she saw in the mirror had somehow been initially distorted, giving an unfair image. Every angle showed the same drawn and tired face. This was her face and tears began to well up in her eyes.

Maybe it was vanity, but she couldn't help but to think of how Moses would react if he saw her now. It had been two years since she last saw him and the past two years had not been kind to her. She thought about love. She thought about the difference between a mother's love for her children and the love a wife had for their husbands. It was an unfair comparison. A mother could never be expected to love a man more than their children. Maybe it was because children were a part of themselves or mothers by some invisible force of God made it so. The two loves were different....but not necessarily less. Just different. But could her love for her children been as strong had not Moses been there? Juliet could see Moses' smile. His affection for the children. She saw him playing and laughing with the children and she saw him comfort the children when they were sick or they had hurt themselves. She saw his God given gentleness that spread like a warm quilt over each and every one of them. Yes. Her love for her children had been enhanced by the presence of Moses in their lives. Together, Moses and she were like two pillars that supported the structure of family and the love housed within. Pull one pillar down and the other would soon follow, crushing those within it's confines. So, maybe that invisible force of God that gave birth to a mother's love of her children had also brought Moses to her to ensure that her children were loved and cared for as God had cleverly designed.

Juliet now realized that the strength of her soul and the perfect love for her children had quietly been fueled by a man named Moses.

Juliet dropped the ragged sliver of mirror and when it hit the hardened clay ground, the glass broke into three ragged pieces. As she looked down at it, her reflection was disjointed and would have been comical had not the truth already been seen. Melancholy and the resulting helplessness drenched her like a cold winter rain.

Chapter 25
Moses

Moses had just come in from eleven hours of hard work in the fields but he still had that ever present smile on his face. Mr. Allen saw him coming in and marveled at the man. His ability to smile regardless of the situation was infectious and Mr. Allen was no exception to it's contagion.

Allen called Moses over and when he arrived in front of his temporary master he said, "Yes, suh?"

"You know your woman, Juliet, is currently not far from here."

Moses' ears suddenly perked up and a curious look came across his face.

Allen continued, "I've been thinking. With your help, I am now ahead of schedule and will have to wait several days before my seed crop gets delivered, so…..maybe you should consider taking these next few days and go see your woman? Now, don't get too excited quite yet. I need to first speak with Bennett and see if he would approve of this visitation."

The grin on Moses' face broadened into the largest smiles that Mr. Allen had ever witnessed, which in turn put a smile on his own face. Contagious indeed.

Allen then said, "I will ride over to Bennett's farm this evening and run this by him. I will let you know what he said first thing in the morning."

Moses couldn't speak, but no words were necessary. Any man or fool could see that Moses was about to burst with joy. He walked away, no….make that floated away on the lightest of clouds, now turning every other step to profusely thank Mr. Allen. Only in these times would any person be so overwhelmed by such a simple act of kindness. A kindness that soon would not be required from any man just to see his own wife. But, these were the times before freedom where a simple right was looked upon as a benevolent favor. The canvas of slavery is painted with multiple hues of demeaning colors that are seldom seen with the human eye, but instead, must be seen with the human heart.

The next morning, Mr. Allen greeted Moses with a smile and a nod of his head. Allen had not only spoken with Bennett, but on his way home had stopped at the McCormick's where Juliet was working and had received McCormick's approval Moses' visit. Everything was now in place. It was time for Moses to begin his short journey to the McCormick farm.

On his walk to see Juliet, Moses stopped to pick some yellow buttercups growing alongside the road. They were nothing more than a weed, but to Moses, they were the most rare and beautiful flower the world had ever known.

_____

Juliet had been working with other slaves clearing a field for future production of crops when she noticed that the others had suddenly stopped and were looking eastward. A black man had just walked over a hill. A very, very large black man with a fistful of buttercups in his massive hand. They weren't sure if they were seeing a vision or an actual person. Juliet stood and turned toward the direction the others were staring. Her heart broke in a million pieces and tears cascaded down her face. It was Moses. Dear, sweet, Moses!

Moses lumbered toward Juliet who had thrown down her axe and was now running as if God himself had placed wings upon her feet. When they met, Moses swept her up in his massive arms and swung her around and around as if she were some little black rag doll.

Laughing, Juliet said, "Now Moses! You put me down! You hear?"

Moses didn't put her down and Juliet had no intention of pressing the subject. She wrapped her arms tightly around Moses' neck and would not have been able to be pried off with a dozen digging irons.

Moses finally set Juliet down and said, "These are for you", as he handed her the buttercups.

Juliet could only softly say, "Oh, Moses........oh Moses. They is the most beautiful thing I ever did seen."

Moses smiled and said, "No dey ain't. You is the most beautiful thing ever seen."

This brought on another stream of tears and choked out "I ain't beautiful no more, Moses."

Moses responded, "You was beautiful from the first day I lay eyes on you. You is beautiful now. And you be beautiful until the day you die."

A small light began to shine in Juliet's soul once again. She now knew that Moses had always been her light.

The other slaves had now protectively encircled the couple and reached out to affectionately touch both Moses and Juliet.

Chapter 26
Between Two Worlds

Harriet and Newton were 6 years old when they first met at Rock Hall. In their young eyes, color did not exist. Harriet was black and Newton was white. All they understood was that which really mattered. Each other…. and that which was inside them where color did not exist. It was natural that the children of slaves and of white slave owners would play together. Everyone knew that as time went on, the play and friendship between a black and a white would….and must, end. But for now, little Harriet and Newton would hold each others hands while running through the fields looking for their next youthful adventure, oblivious to the rules of society.

Newton's mother was the sister of Bennett, and like most of Bennett's sisters, they tended to congregate several days a week at Bennett's home, knitting, needle pointing, darning clothes, making butter and all assortment of duties that were expected from the women folk. For Bennett's sisters it was more social than work. Their children, too young yet to work, were brought along with them, much to the glee of the children. Here they would play with their cousins as well as the children of Juliet who were not yet expected to do much else than the occasional chores every child performed, regardless of race. Newton's cousin, Jesse Newton Russell, was one year younger than Newton Everhart and Harriet was one year older than Newton. It wasn't long before the three of them became inseparable.

Harriet became the defacto leader of their group by virtue of her age and the fact that she was always challenging the boys to race, throw rocks at an old can, climbing trees or any other games of skill she could come up with….other than swimming. In the beginning none of them could swim and they stayed away from the old pond beyond the hills north of the house. As the years went on, both boys learned to swim and they egged Harriet on to join them in the pond. Nothing frustrated her as much as not being able to do everything the boys could do and to actually do it better than the boys. Sometimes, when the boys went swimming, she would stand on the shore and throw rocks at them. Not because she was angry with them but she knew it would chase them from the water and in turn, chase her….where she could be included in the fun. After several minutes of unsuccessfully trying to catch her, they would all lie down exhausted, laughing and threatening to throw Harriet in the pond where she would reply that they had to catch her first and then adding that they had a better chance of catching a lighting bolt! The good natured ribbing would go back and forth for a while before they were off on another adventure. But, learning to swim never was far from her mind, yet, she was deathly afraid of the water. It really didn't matter to Harriet if she could swim or not. As she always told the boys, "If God wanted me to be a fish, then He wuda made me a fish." And with that, more teasing would always follow.

   Whenever Harriet brought up swimming to Juliet, she was told in no uncertain terms to stay away from that pond. That people drowned around these parts everyday! That of course wasn't true, but Juliet wanted to make sure she got Harriet's attention. Harriet would lower her head and nod, but beneath the surface, she was galled by the fact that these two boys could do something she couldn't.

———————————————————

When Newton arrived at Rock Hall one day, he was told that Jesse had ridden to Winchester with his father, Bennett, and would not be back until later in the day. Although disappointed that his favorite cousin wasn't there, his disappointment was short lived knowing that he still had Harriet to go with him on a new adventure.

Harriet was usually nearby waiting for Newton when he arrived, but today, she was no where in sight. After asking about here whereabouts, one of Harriet's sisters, Amanda, told him that she thought she had seen Harriet walking out through the fields. When Newton asked Harriet which direction was she headed, Amanda pointed to the hills off to the north exactly where the pond could be found just down slope of the hills.

Newton immediately, and with some trepidation, followed up on the only hint of her whereabouts and headed north to the hills that led to the pond on the other side.

The land here held more hills that flat land and each hill was dotted with limestone outcrops, black walnut trees and the ever present locust tree. The hills and rock outcrops made farming more difficult but the soils found here were perfectly suited for growing wheat, and wheat was the Shenandoah Valley's cash crop that enabled a poor man to become a rich man. This slender valley was less than 25 miles wide at this point, with visible mountain ranges to the east and west. Certainly, the limestone laden valley presented it's own unique challenges to farming, but it more than made up for this geological trait with some of the most fertile soils to be found anywhere in the state of Virginia. Combined with the soils and the favorable climate that produced both hardwood and softwood trees of nearly all varieties, it's indigenous blue grass that made for the best grazing in the country along with it's incredible wealth of water sources, Clarke

County was both an agrarian and aesthetic paradise.

As Newton crested the northern hills he could look down on the pond. There he saw a lone figure along the pond's shore. There was little or no movement and he began to run.

When Newton reached the pond, Harriet looked up and smiled. His fear now turned to anger. As so often it was, fear, then relief, was so often followed by pointless anger. Newton's chest was heaving from his race to the pond and exacerbated by the fear he felt when he first saw Harriet's stillness by the pond's edge.

Newton now stood before Harriet and verbally lashed her. She sat looking up at him with both surprise and hurt painted on a face that had become that of neither a child or a woman.

When Newton had vented his fear induced anger and had nothing left inside him, he sat down beside her and absent mindlessly began tossing rocks into the pond, avoiding facing her. No one said a word for several minutes before Newton finally said, "I was so scared. I thought something had happened to you."

Harriet remained quiet but slipped her hand into his. She understood that his anger had been borne out of deep concern for her safety. Newton sheepishly turned his head toward her and then the most surprising and life changing moment occurred. Harriet leaned forward and kissed Newton.

Newton initially drew back like most 12 year old boys would do, but then leaned back into Harriet and returned her kiss. He never wanted to release her small delicate hand ever again. They both smiled and they both experienced a new and wonderful reason for a smile. For Newton, it all seemed so strange, but it was a strangeness that he would fall asleep to that night…..with a small smile on his face.

The moment was suddenly broken when Harriet exclaimed, "Look what I found, Newton!"

She reached into a pocket that had been sewn on her dress from mismatched fragment of another cloth and pulled out two old coins.

They had been tarnished with age and the elements of the ground, but writing, a partially exposed date and a symbol could still be seen on them. The language could not be deciphered by Newton but the symbol on the coin showed two hands joined together. He had seen a symbol similar to this once before on a ring that an Irishman wore on one of his fingers.

Harriet took one of the coins out of her palm and held it toward Newton and said, "Yours. We will each keep one for life."

And so they did.

Chapter 27
New Day, New Lawyer
1854

Winchester was much larger than Berryville and with the increased population, came increased crowds. All fighting for a place inside the courthouse. Outside of the courthouse, it had taken on the atmosphere of a festival. Hard cider was being offered to the adults and hard candy to the children. Household wares of all kinds were being sold from the back of wagons and ragged little children sold apples that they had stolen the night before. Men dressed in a mismatch of clothing that made a vain attempt at professionalism, but upon closer inspection, had been patched and small rips hastily sewn. These charlatans of medicine hawked miracle elixirs that cured every possible ailment imaginable, and even some aliments not yet imagined.

The circus had returned and with it, every conceivable freak show imaginable.

After a year and a half of postponements and delaying tactics by Williams, Conrad finally had his chance to prove himself in front of the largest courtroom scene in his career. Publicity of this magnitude appealed to the ambitious nature of Conrad but it also created a slippery slope. He needed to present himself as one of the state's leading legal authorities without upsetting the slave owning men who could help him reach the lofty perch of social standing and respectability. Having chosen to walk a fine line between the two worlds, he would have to exercise caution. This went against his natural inclination, but if he won the case for Juliet, he himself could lose the support of a wealthy and prominent slave owning class whose influence would be necessary in his personal advancement. He now found himself in what was called a conundrum. A conundrum of his own choosing.

Initially, Conrad had planned, rightfully so, to contest the request by Williams to have this man Spurr be allowed to testify to *abstentia* regarding the witnessing of the Articles of Agreement. He knew that if the court agreed to this, then his ability to cross examine Spurr would be forfeited and therefore allowing Williams to dictate the outcome. Regardless, Conrad decided not to argue this highly unfair request by Williams. It would go unnoticed to most in the court, other than to those slave owners who had never been comfortable with a man like Spurr on the witness stand. Conrad had no doubt that Spurr could be broken in a number of ways if cross examined which would cast doubt, not only on a key witness, but the entire suit brought by Bennett Russell. He relished the idea of confronting Spurr, but if that particular moment of cross examination happened to lead to courtroom victory for him, it could also result in a loss of those prominent and powerful friends he had been cultivating for his own rise in prominence and power.

Conrad had taken the first cautious step on a hazardous slope made slick with competing values.

Today, Juliet walked into the strange new courthouse in Winchester with her signature red scarf tied neatly over her head, but this time she was accompanied by her husband, Moses. The two of them drew the normal stares that Juliet had become somewhat accustomed to, but Moses was new to this strange new world and it showed. Juliet, as usual, stood erect and defiant. Moses stood wide eyed with uncertainty and fear, that stood in stark contrast to his enormous physical stature, which made many who saw him for the first time, react in similar fashion. Had they known his gentleness, they would have reacted in an entirely different manner.

Due to his extraordinary height, his pants ended well above his ankles. His shirt struggled unsuccessfully to cover the upper part of his chest, making the last 3 buttons of his shirt no more than mere decorations spaced widely apart from one another. This only had the effect of making him appear to be more gigantic than he already was. No shirt ever fit Moses. His massive arms and shoulders would rip the stitching where the sleeves met his shoulders and therefore out of necessity, his arms would always remain bare, as they did today. The women who attended court this day were more fascinated than frightened of Moses' physique and stared at him in what some might describe as in a curiously unholy manner. They would all gather later to convince each other, as well as themselves, that they had bee so frightened at his appearance, that they could not take their eyes off him. Apparently, some women had been so *frightened* of similarly built black men that their *fear* made them take temporary leave of their senses and drove them *unconsciously* into the arms of their slaves. Fear, it would seem, worked in quite peculiar ways for some of these *innocent* flowers of the South.

After everyone was seated, or were forced to stand due to the overcrowding of the courtroom, the judge brought order to the court. He then summarized for the jury the particulars of the suit brought by Bennett Russell against Juliet in an attempted to bring the jury up to date as best he could. The judge was new. The jury new. And the attorney for Juliet was new. This made for a slow and at times, a chaotic scene, with all the new faces either straining to understand or continually referring to their notes. Philip Williams needed no tutoring. Only he and Juliet knew what had gone before, and Juliet being a slave, had no say in the matter. Williams sat back in his chair absentmindedly inspecting his fingernails, quietly enjoying his advantage.

Juliet was more than a little concerned, and rightfully so. The change in venue had in effect taken the case back to square one. But more importantly, she had been strapped with a new lawyer to represent her. The attorney, Robert Conrad, did not have the same rapport or calming effect on her like Richard Parker had, had. To top things off, her money was quickly running out in which to pay an attorney. The combination of all these elements left her uneasy, to say the least. A storm that initially threatened her quest for freedom at the onset of the trial had been kept at bay by the legally astute counter winds of Parker's relentless attack on the Articles of Agreement. Now, the sky once again darkened for Juliet. It wasn't all Conrad's fault. He had been put in the difficult, if not impossible, position of effectively carrying on a case that had already proceeded for 3 years without him. At no fault of her own, she was in essence changing a wheel on a moving wagon.

Williams stood and asked to approach the bench, but not before the judge warned, "You may approach the bench, Mr Williams, but make it pertinent to this trial and to the laws of this state."

"Your Honor", spoke Williams, "I believe that the court has been made aware of the difficulty in having Mr. Spurr personally attend and provide his testimony."

Conrad had been expecting this and knew what was coming next.

Williams continued, "Mr. Spurr is a traveling saddler in which his profession takes him many miles from our present location. We have only recently been able to make contact with Mr. Spurr and he is at least a 4 days ride from Winchester. His ride here, his testimony and his ride back would easily take at least 10 days out of Mr. Spurr's time. There is no one who would rather have Mr. Spurr here than the plaintiff, Mr. Bennett Russell, himself. Mr. Spurr, on the other hand, has a wife and family to feed and care for. For Mr. Spurr to take 10 days of his time to come here to testify would be a great hardship not only for Mr. Spurr, but more importantly, the hardship would fall more directly upon the shoulders of a frail wife and their children. It is therefore, my hope and prayer that the court would consider my request that a written document to the effect of his witnessing of Mr. Crafton's Articles of Agreement be mailed to Mr. Spurr to sign in the presence of a duly sworn official in Mr. Spurr's jurisdiction as would be acceptable to this court."

The request to have Spurr testify through the mail had not come as a surprise to Conrad. Although, he had wondered why any saddler would take his business on the road in such sparsely populated areas, far from any center of human activity when he could make three times what he most certainly be making in the hills of far western Virginia. His instincts told him that Spurr had chosen a remote area not because it was physically safe, which it surely was not, but more likely because it was safe from the law. He had no way in which to prove that Spurr was one of those men who fled the law to find refuge in the backwater of Virginia. To make such a declaration without proof, would hardly be the best way to endear himself to the judge.

Conrad then asked the judge if he could approach the bench and his request was likewise granted.

Conrad then said, "Your Honor, the defense is not unsympathetic to the plight of Mr. Spurr's family, although, the defense requests that should the request by the plaintiff's attorney be accepted by this court, that we reserve the right to cross examine Mr. Spurr at a later time, should indeed Mr. Spurr be struck with the urge to testify in person or should find himself in convenient proximity of his Honor's court."

The judge pondered the two request by the plaintiff's and defense's attorneys before making a decision.

"Although, it is highly irregular that a critical witness to any case not to personally attend the court to testify, and for the witness not be able to be cross examined by the other party as a result of the reasons presented by the plaintiff, it is my opinion to allow for Mr. Spurr's testimony to be given in writing and witnessed by an attorney of good standing in the jurisdiction in which Mr. Spurr is residing. Furthermore, as the defense has pointed out, the ability to cross examine the witness should be reserved for the defense should indeed Mr. Spurr be in a position to testify in person. Therefore, it is the ruling of this court to allow for written testimony by Mr. Spurr, but the court also will require that the plaintiff's attorney not to commence the process of having Mr. Spurr's testimony requested through mail until he has exhausted every effort to have Mr. Spurr testify in person by the next session of the court so as to provide the opportunity for the defense to cross examine Mr. Spurr. If Mr. Spurr is still unable of testify in person, then this court will allow for written testimony, but not until after the next term of court. I therefore postpone court until the next regularly scheduled court session.

Court is hereby adjourned."

The dark cloud over Juliet and her struggle for freedom remained. Ominous and suffocating. Neither Moses or she had testified. Nor would they. A slave's testimony was prohibited by law, and even if it was allowed, it would carry next to nothing in weight. They were only there as a quirk of the law that required both the defendant and the plaintiff to attend court. Bennett Russell was able to give his account but Juliet could not. She stood on a tilted playing field with her feet sunken in quicksand that was quickly threatening to swallow her whole.

Conrad walked from the courtroom, stopping to shake hands and speak with those more affluent spectators who had attended today's court. Each praised him for conditional acceptance of the plaintiff's request that Spurr be allowed to testify by mail, saying they believed that he had made a worthy compromise which would preserve his right to cross examine Spurr at a later date. They all knew that a later date would never come. It was in it's own simplicity, a minor stroke of genius. Conrad saved face with his request to reserve the right to examine Spurr on the witness stand, while at the same time pleasing those who could further his career. He even had caught out of the side of his eye, Bennett Russell nodding his head in approval. Certainly those with even greater wealth and larger slave ownership would come to the same conclusion. All in all, a successful day in court.

Life, as it was, continued to physically and emotionally take it's withering toll on Juliet and Moses.

Chapter 28
A Step Closer?

A series of stalling tactics had been successfully used by Williams during the last three court sessions. In many ways, he was amazed that he had not bankrupted Juliet before now. Conrad had no choice to make it clear to Philips Williams that he was ready to rest his case. She had no choice in the matter. Broke and unable to pay an attorney, it was time to let the chips fall where they may.

The initial case made by Parker was still a strong case and Conrad had surprised Juliet in his follow up and tenacity. Although, Spurr had never personally attended court to testify and be cross examined by Conrad, Spurr's son had recently been charged with a murder and convicted. Conrad had used this bit of information to help cast more doubt on the character of Spurr. Williams rightfully objected when Conrad brought up the subject and the judge had rightfully sustained the objection. But, another seed had been planted in the jury's minds. Conrad noticed that the jurors were looking at one another and quietly speaking to their neighbor in the jury box. The judge brought order to the court after this bit of damaging news and reprimanded the jurors for discussing that which could not and would not be tolerated in a court of law.

The dark cloud that had hoovered stubbornly over Juliet the past several years had lightened ever so much and for the first time in years, she felt that tingle of hope. However slight it may have been. She was a realist and therefore quickly pushed away this feeling of hope for fear that it would heartlessly turn on her, vanquishing hope and leaving her in despair. She lived in a white man's world and her fate was in the hands of 12 white men of the jury. If that alone did not temper her hope, then she was a fool. Juliet was no fool.

Chapter 29
Hard Reflection

Now a respected judge, Richard E. Parker sat on his expansive veranda overlooking the river he had always loved, and reflected on his life. On his victories. And on the mistakes he had made in life. As child, he had spent his summers exploring up and down the river, finding ancient Indian arrow heads, learning to swim and fish, swinging from a rope and dropping into the deep cool waters of the Shenandoah. Tonight, the river was calm as it usually was, but the old river could be deceiving below the surface. Still waters run deep and the dangers there are often unseen until it was too late.

Parker had been following the case of his former clients, Juliet and her family. He now wondered whether his ploy of starting gossip about the witness William Spurr to get a short term advantage had in fact backfired in favor of Philip Williams in the long term. It was no doubt in his mind, that his manufactured gossip had eventually reached Spurr, and if Spurr had indeed something in his past to hide, then it surely would have pushed Spurr deeper into the relative safety of the backwoods of western Virginia. If Spurr had a criminal past, then there would be no way that Spurr would show up at the trial to testify. Barring any sudden changes in Spurr's desire to remain hidden, Conrad would be at the disadvantage of not being able to question Spurr under the intense scrutiny of cross examination. Both Conrad and Williams knew that a man like Spurr could be lured into traps that would destroy his credibility as a witness. Putting Spurr on the witness stand could be the difference in Juliet winning her freedom or not.

Tactical law, like the river, had hidden depths and dangers. Parker felt as if he had not listened to the lessons of the river and now had an uneasy feeling that Juliet could be swept under it's currents as a direct result of his error in judgment.

As darkness fell, he remained motionless on his veranda, other than the unconscious, slow stroking of his hands, much like a loving mother would do for their child in an attempt to soothe away their pain. But the uneasy pain remained and no amount of hand wringing would change that.

Chapter 30
The Verdict
1856

The day had finally, and mercifully come to announce the verdict. It had been 8 torturous years. Juliet was 33 years old when the battle for her freedom began. She was now 41 years old, drawn and exhausted. The toll on Juliet had left her once black hair a solid white. Eight years of carrying the burden of legal battle and 8 years of family separation as was required by the court, had left Juliet slightly stooped and her movements slow like a woman twice her age. For many, she was only recognizable by her faded red scarf wound tightly around her head. The last vestige of pride.

Her attorney, Robert Conrad, had watched this once strong and proud woman meta-morph into the woman who stood all but broken beside him today. He had not realized until today that the events of the last 5 years on this now frail woman, had also taken an emotional toll on him. He had come to respect this woman in a way he had never thought possible. More than that, he had come to question the entire institution of slavery. For the first time in his life, he saw slavery through the eyes of a slave and what he saw shook his entire life long view on slavery. What he saw standing with him today was more than a slave. She was a person of flesh and blood, no different from himself, other than she was black and had the misfortune of being born a slave.

It was no secret that today the attorneys would give their closing arguments and the jury would make their decision. The courtroom and courthouse grounds were filled like no other time during the trial. The final act was about to commence and the circus atmosphere was thick and alive with it's own unique form of electricity.

When order in the court was finally achieved, Williams, the attorney for "Bennett Russell and Others", rose from his chair and approached the jury to give his closing argument.

"Gentlemen of the jury, I appreciate your service to our community. It has been a long, drawn out case but the facts remain exactly as they were from the beginning of this trial. Relying on these facts can only lead each of you to render a verdict that accepts the Articles of Agreement as the *true* last will and testament of John Russell Crafton.

There has been no evidence given by the defense that would lead to any other conclusion. Every witness to the signing of the Articles of Agreement by John Russell Crafton has testified under oath that the directives in the Articles revoking the subject slave's freedom was indeed the last wishes of Mr. Crafton.

The defense has attempted to sow doubt in your minds but there has not been any evidentiary argument that has proven their loose and wildly speculative attempt to have you believe that there was foul play. Indeed, sirs, the defense's argument could easily be considered slanderous to a well respected family of a county that only recently had been a part of our own proud county. Many of you on the jury today know Bennett Russell and know that he has never once broken the law and has, along with his entire family, been one of our community's most prominent and law abiding citizens in the entire area. Only weeks ago, Bennett Russell was elected as a Gentleman Justice to Clarke County. *Gentleman. Justice.* These two words, if you knew nothing more about Mr. Bennett Russell, should be everything you need to know regarding the character of Mr. Russell. One is not elected to such a lofty position of the law if one is neither a *gentleman* or a man who values and understands *justice.* Not to find for the plaintiff would indeed be one of the greatest *injustices* in modern times.

I close with my appreciation and compliment to each of you for giving your valuable time to this matter and feel confident that one of the most intelligent juries that I have ever seen assembled, will indeed come to the obvious conclusion, that the Articles of Agreement is the legal last will and testament of John Russell Crafton."

Conrad paused before rising and addressing the jury, quietly tapping his finger on his desk. The courtroom had become so quiet, that most could actually hear Conrad's nearly indistinct tapping. Conrad rose, walked towards the jury with his head lowered in thought and his hand lifted and finger slightly wagging indicating that he did not buy what Williams had just stated and was about to tell the jury exactly why Williams' conclusion was wrong.

Conrad stood before the jury and scanned every juror's face before beginning his closing argument. Making eye contact with each juror was a subtle conveyance of his legal and moral authority, not unlike a pastor before his flock. He gave the stern impression that he knew what they were thinking, while at the same time silently scolding them for having been duped into accepting Williams' argument. A risky move. A lawyer normally wanted the jury to like them and bond with them. This was no longer a time for bonding and certain risks must be taken. He needed to have the juror's minds cleared of the last words they heard and be open to his argument.

"Gentlemen of the jury. The plaintiff's attorney would attempt to convince you of the simplicity of the law. The law is, as all of you know, anything but simple. Within the law itself, those who sit in judgment must understand complexities of both the law and human weaknesses."

Conrad then reached within his jacket and pulled out a bible for all to see and stated, "As the Holy Bible tells us, man is continually tempted and has been since the days of Adam and Eve. Man is tempted by a host of sins but the temptation of money, can and does, drive many men to do questionable things. More often than not, these are not bad persons. They are only weak and therefore led down a path of sin, but we must not condemn these persons for their human frailty, but must instead save them from themselves. Bennett Russell and his family are not bad people. They are only like the rest of us who have in their lives temporarily strayed from the path of righteousness. Today, each of you on the jury have the power to save Bennett and his family the guilty pleasure of ill gotten gains."

Conrad further expounded, "Why do I, like so many others, believe that the plaintiff's have veered from the path of righteousness? Let me remind each of you what we already know. We know that it was the wish of John Russell Crafton to free his slaves and the will was written when Mr. Crafton was of sound mind and body. It has been proven that prior to these so called Articles of Agreement being signed, Mr. Crafton had suffered a stroke that effected both his body and his mind. He had become incapable of even buttoning his shirt, much less, signing his name. It was not Mr. Crafton's signature that you saw on the Articles of Agreement, but instead, *his mark made as an "X"*. A child would be able to draw an "X" and therefore easily forge any document.

Secondly, every single witness to these Articles of Agreement were those who stood to benefit from the revocation of the slave's freedom, save a man by the name of Mr. Spurr, who all but disappeared and never testified in person before the jury thus casting further doubt on the legitimacy of the witnesses as a whole and particularly on Mr. Spurr. Mr. Williams considers everything the defense has presented as wild speculation. It is not one degree of speculation when I say that against all norms of law that those who would benefit from the revocation of the slave's freedom *signed* as witnesses to the Articles of Agreement. I have practiced law for over 20 years and not once have I seen a will of this nature signed by family members who would benefit. Wills, as each of you know, are kept away from view from family members and the public for a purpose. If indeed anyone could read a man's will prior to it being probated, then directives within a will could easily not only be disputed by an heir, but be destroyed or amended by a disgruntled beneficiary. For some reason, this norm regarding the privacy of one's will was not followed, and you as jurors, need to see if there was anything that would have made Bennett and his family not follow the norms of the law. The slaves in question have a value of $12,000! The same value of 400 acres of prime farmland. Not a small amount of money! And money makes even the best of people do things they would not otherwise do. The norms of laws governing wills were broken…...if not shattered.

Lastly, was it speculation when it was shown that the Articles of Agreement did not legally state that it revoked all wills and last testaments that had come before it? It is not speculation that the Articles did omit the one simple fact and directive as legally required in all wills. No attorney would have ever made this mistake and it further shows that the plaintiffs had not wanted an attorney to draw up the Articles of Agreement as they were fully aware that no attorney would have taken part in such a fraudulent scheme!

In closing, I also want to thank the jury for their selfless service to the law and I enjoin each of you to see through the fog of corruption and follow a path that supersedes all of man's laws and follow the ultimate laws of our Lord while also following the laws of this state."

With closing arguments made by both sides, the judge ordered the jury to be removed to a room to make their decision. Court was then recessed until the jury returned with a verdict.

Juliet was removed from the court and taken to a jail cell for her own protection. There, she knelt, and looking skyward placed her hands together in prayer. There was no need to overhear what she was asking the Lord. The jail keepers knew without question what her heavenly plea was requesting.

She remained on her knees for 6 hours when the jailer unlocked her cell and told her that the jury had returned with their verdict. The jailer saw that she was struggling to get to her feet and went to her. Anyone who could remain in prayer on her knees, on a hard cold floor for 6 hours straight, deserved both respect and a helping hand, regardless of his own personal views on slavery.

The 6 hours that the jury had been sequestered indicated that they had wrestled with a verdict, but had apparently overcome any potential deadlock and now notified the bailiff sitting outside their room that they had reached a decision and were ready to return to the courtroom. The word spread like a wind swept fire in a field of dry wheat shafts that the jury had reached a decision and were filing into the courtroom. Many of the spectators were now drunk from having sat in a tavern for 6 hours and some jumped to their feet so quickly that they literally passed out and fell across their table to be left as they were. The mad dash to the courthouse looked like a mob of drunken sailors on board a ship in rough waters. Lurching and falling as they attempted to outrace the other.

When order was restored in the court, the judge stated, "Gentleman of the jury, how do you find in the case Bennett Russell and Others vs. Negroes Juliet and Others?"

The foreman of the jury rose and loudly proclaimed, "Your Honor. We find in favor of the plaintiff in the case of Bennett Russell and Others vs. Negroes Juliet and Others."

Juliet had lost and with it, her family.

In one short burst, the judge struck his gavel and ordered, "Court is now adjourned!"

There were actually cheers that went up in the courtroom and hands being shaken all around. Bennett was being patted on the back, hands pushing through the crowd towards Bennett to shake his hand and be congratulated on his well earned victory. The court had an atmosphere of joviality and headiness.

Bennett was being given celebrity status, and although he was pleased with the outcome, he took no real joy in winning. Juliet's family would now be separated and sold. There was no satisfaction in separating a family for what might be and likely be forever. If there was one thing he could do, it would be to have the entire family sold as one unit to one owner. But, that he knew, never occurred at slave auctions. They would be sold one by one. Some may actually end up with a buyer who had earlier purchased one of the slave's family members, but that would be as close as it would get to the family remaining together. Bennett was a hard man, but not a heartless man.

Bennett had done what he had done, not so much for his personal benefit, but for the benefit of his family. He had no doubt, had Juliet been in his place, she would have done the same. To a parent, and to one who was responsible to their entire family, one did what was in the best interest of the family.

Occasionally, those decisions could have consequences that, instead of instilling satisfaction, left one feeling a sense of emptiness. It was a hollow man who now walked purposely to his carriage. Leaving the circus behind.

Juliet walked in agony to the carriage of Thomas Gold, who had transported her to the trial today. Although Gold was a slave owner and had celebrated the verdict today, he had lost that initial excitement as he sat beside Juliet. He tried to convince himself that there was no shame in celebrating today's verdict, but then, why did he feel shame? Not a word was spoken between Juliet and himself on the entire hour and half ride back home. There were no words for today's events that could be spoken with Juliet. The trip back home seemed like it would never end and he was grateful when he finally came in sight of Bennett's farm.

Though Juliet would not allow herself to show any emotion that might be construed as weakness or defeat on the ride home, hidden inside her was a virtual cyclone of emotion that was uprooting the very core of her being. Her heart had been hurled through the swirling winds of emotion and was irreparably splintered into shards of grief against the hardness of reality. If there could be anything positive retrieved from this wreckage, it was that now that the verdict had been rendered, Juliet and her family were no longer bound to the court order to remove them from Bennett's farm. For the time being, they would all be able to reunite for the first time in 8 years. Hopelessness, sadness, fear, uncertainty and joy would swirl through each one of them, creating a turgid flood of competing emotions.

As Juliet walked towards the slave quarters, she lifted her head and restored her once proud posture. Her family needed her strong and needed her to help them through the days to come. But, as she neared the doorway and heard the voices of those she had loved more than herself, tears she had sought so hard to hold back, ran freely down her cheeks.

Juliet walked through the leather hinged door where the others waited, opening her arms wide in an invitation for all her family to unite as one through love. The tears of their affection for both Juliet and each other were sprinkled upon the other like a baptism releasing them from the pain of their earthly world.

———————————————————————

The final written opinion and order by the judge and jury was entered into the court at Clarke County on the 12th day of May, 1856 and read as follows:

The issue "Devisant vel non" heretofore awarded in this case and the cause with the trial of said issue naming been removed to the Circuit Court of the county of Frederick by an order of this court made on the 14th day of October, 1851. Upon the return of said papers from said causes from the said Circuit Court of Frederick. This day came the parties by their attorneys and the Prossounders (?) by their attorney produced the verdict and the judgment enclosed theron by the said Circuit Court of Frederick County as follows to wit: the verdict; We the jury find from the evidence of Thomas W. Russell, William R. Spurr, John W. Russell it being the evidence relied upon that John Russell, Sr. did execute the paper in the above issue named there being no evidence in the minds of the jury to disprove it. We therefore find the said paper writing to be the last will and testament of John Russell, Sr. dec. Zephemiah

Silvers, Foreman, "And the judgment as follows to wit: Therefore, it is considered by the court that the said paper

*writing in the issue named, marked, "The Articles of Agreement"
be established and recorded as the Last Will and Testament of
John Russell, Sr. dec. and that the finding of the jury and the
order of the court be certified to the Circuit Court of Clarke
County where the said John Russell lived up to the time of his
death. The will having been offered for probate in the Circuit
Superior Court of Law and Chancery for Clarke County that the
original will and other papers be returned to the Circuit Court of
Clarke County that the said will be recorded.*

*It is therefore ordered that the said papers marked Articles of
Agreement be recorded as the Last Will and Testament of John
Russell, Sr. dec. and there being no executor named in said will,
on the motion of Bennett Russell administrator of the estate of
said John Russell, Sr. dec. with the will annexed and granted to
him on his entering into bond with security, whereupon he, with
Benjamin Morgan (who justified under oath as to his sufficiency)
entered into and acknowledged bond in the penalty of Thirty
Thousand Dollars conditioned that he shall faithfully discharge
the duties of his said office of administrator aforesaid. It is
further ordered that, that all original papers of title be made
exhibits in this cause may be taken therefrom by the persons
legally entitled to them. Upon there being copies thereof to be
made and attested by the clerk of this court and any other such
papers, deeds, and other evidences of title, now among the papers
and not of exhibits in this cause may be delivered to the persons
entitled to their possession without such copies being made or
left. It is ordered that Josiah J. Janney, William D. Smith, John
Burchell, Thomas E. Gold, Stephen Gant and Mann R. Page or
any three of them being duly sworn do appraise the slaves if any
and personal estate of John Russell, Sr. dec. in the hands of
Bennett Russell his admin. with the will annexed and make report
thereon to this court.*

Teste

D. McGuire

The storm, that had for so long threatened Juliet, had finally struck and carried her away in nothing more than paper, words and ink.

Chapter 32
Marshall's Last Chance

Marshall had remained silent since the verdict, but his family knew that his silence had not meant resignation to his continued bondage. Quite the opposite. Harriet, more than the others, knew Marshall. They were only one year apart in age and their love and friendship for one another had never once faded in all the years together. Harriet use to lead Marshall around by her hand from the time Marshall could walk. They played together, shared secrets together and at night shared the same bed together. They had become inseparable and knew one another as well as they understood themselves, if not better. Harriet knew what was going on inside Marshall and she feared what she knew.

When Harriet and Marshall were alone, she asked him, "What's goin' on inside yo head, Marshall? Don't lie to me. You know I knows you."

Marshall looked at Harriet with both sadness and determination but never said a word.

"You runnin' ain't you?" asked Harriet.

Again, Marshall said nothing.

Harriet sagged for a moment and said, "Please, Marshall. Don't do it! We don't know what will happen. If we be sold, maybe we be sold together."

Even Harriet didn't believe her last words, but she was afraid that if Marshall ran away, and then was caught, the consequences could be devastating for Marshall. She was trying to save Marshall from himself, but also understood his desire to escape. The verdict at court had been devastating to each of them and all were filled with dread and desperation.

"You knows I can't stay. Not as no slave," declared Marshall.

Marshall and Harriet were 18 and 19 years old respectively. Both prime age, and as brother and sister, she knew that they would be sold separately and used as breeders and well as slave labor. Harriet tried to push the thought from her head and in doing so, she understood Marshall and could not bring herself to stand in his way. It was a risk worth taking. For her, she would not take the risk. There was a young man in the area the same age as herself and they had begun to secretly see one another. She could only hope that she would be sold to someone nearby so that she and her young man might still be able to see each other. She was pregnant with his child and even if she had wanted to escape, it would have been no longer possible for her. In her condition, running was out of the question.

The next morning, Marshall was gone. Marshall would bring the highest price of all the slaves, so Bennett Russell had acted swiftly to put out a sizable reward for his capture and return. Every bounty hunter and man down on his luck, took up the challenge of finding Marshall. It hadn't taken long. He was found 2 days later in a barn in Jefferson County. The owner of the small farm had heard his hounds barking and found them at the barn door leaping and scratching at the faded gray wooden plank doors accompanied by the hound's excitable cries.

Marshall was led out at gun point and taken directly to the jail in Charles Town. This time, Bennett took no chances. Marshall was immediately placed in leg irons and his wrist rudely chained together.

He would remain that way until a week before the auction. His unshackling was not the act of compassion, but was done in order to provide time for the marks of his capture to fade. Regardless of whether a male slave was in his prime or not, marks of having been chained had a tendency to scare some bidders away and thus reduce the bidding which would then have a direct result on the sale price. He was locked securely in a makeshift jail in the old corn crib until the day of the auction. There, Marshall considered his fate nearly every waking hour. None of which was good.

Chapter 33
Eve of the Auction

The night before the auction, Juliet and all her family met at Harriet's quarters. Years before, Moses had meticulously carved out a cross from a single piece of old tree stump and then hung it from a wall in Juliet's and his quarters. On this night, he solemnly removed the cross and carried it to their meeting place. The Lord had always been the shelter of hope and salvation of their family. They were no different from all slave families who had little in life in which to rejoice and Christ had given them that one small thread of hope and celebration. Within that simple wooden cross was a hidden power that lifted their fading hopes. They all reverently huddled near the cross tonight and prayed for the strength to see them through tomorrow's sorrow. Juliet knew that she must say something to give her family comfort. Fleeting as it may be. The challenge to provide hope where none existed, seemed an impossible task.

She walked up to the cross and laid her hands on it with the hope that God would give life to her tongue and then turned to her family.

"We is the children of God almighty and He will walk with us, no matter the distance. No matter the danger. No matter how long the journey. God has spoken to me and He says that our journey will be only for a little time more and for us to believe in Him and know that freedom is comin' for us. We has all suffered and we's gonna suffer a little while longer. But he says "Don't give up, chiluns! Your time will come!" He tell me too, that he done gave us life and a brain. Each of you must use your brains.

To not use what God gave you is a sin. To not always try is a sin.
To not continue the struggle is a sin. We have tried mightily in
our struggles these past 8 years but it ain't the end. No suh! It
ain't the end."

Juliet paused. She had nothing more to say…....save one thing.

"If you don't jump in the pond, you nevuh gonna swim".
Don't none of you ever forget that! NEVUH!"

That night they did not go to their separate quarters, but
remained together as one, sleeping wherever space could be
found. Tonight, comfort would be found in the nearness to one
another.

Chapter 34
The Auction

Juliet and her family were led out and one by one made to stand on the back of a flat bed wagon so that the crowds who had gathered to purchase slaves that day could get a better look at their potential purchases.

Juliet would be the first to go on the block. Marshall would be second. It was no surprise to see that the two who had created the most problems for the Russell family were the first to be sold. The locals wanted no part of either one, so the bids that came in, were from those who had traveled some distance to attend the auction. Both would be taken far from their family members and both had stared vacantly down at the floor of the wagon, unable and unwilling to see those who furiously bid on them, comfortable within their own hazy morality.

Before Juliet was led to the makeshift auction block she wondered if she would have a chance to see her family before being separated for life. To hug them. Touch them. To be able to sear their faces into her memory forever. One last bittersweet goodbye.

Several hours before the auction had began, Juliet stood outside with her arm around Harriet. Together they smelled the sweet fragrance of a plant they called Licorice Weed. Juliet remembered when Harriet was a little girl and couldn't understand why her mother wouldn't let her pick and eat this delightfully smelling plant. She then remembered turning away from Harriet for just a moment and hearing the little girl spitting furiously to rid her mouth of this bitter tasting weed that lured all children to it's scent. She remembered laughing while reaching down to wipe Harriet's mouth and then lovingly consoling her in her arms. Forever she would remember.

Harriet had been introduced to licorice one Christmas years ago when old man Crafton had brought them each a licorice stick. All the children had devoured their treat in a matter of minutes, but Harriet, so taken by it's taste, had never wanted it to end. For weeks she would take out her stick and slowly savor each small and calculated lick before it finally disappeared altogether. She had cried as the last hard bit of it dissolved in her mouth.

Juliet's mind could barely keep up with the onslaught of memories of her children and of Moses. Sweet Moses. She prayed that she and Moses would be sold together. She feared that if they weren't sold together, that he would just walk off one day and lie down by some stream shattered and heartbroken, where he would will his own death to carry him softly away into the currents of time.

Moses was the next *item* on the auction block. Like a dying man, his life flashed before him. A lifetime of memories galloping through his mind in slow motion. He remembered the first time he had laid eyes of Juliet. He was only 14 years old at the time, but due to his great size, he appeared much older. Juliet was 5 years older than Moses and wasn't for several more years before she found out how old Moses actually was.

Moses had been working loading up one of the wagons when John Russell Crafton pulled in with his other wagon. Instead of being loaded with goods, was a young, and what some people might describe as haughty, black woman. Her neck was slender and her features sharp, unlike his own. Her unique beauty had actually cowered him into dropping his eyes, yet he couldn't help but occasionally stealing a furtive glance her way. When Crafton and this strange woman walked up to him, he was told that she would be working with him and her name was *Juliet*. Though he had wanted to speak, his tongue would not respond and so all he did was put out his hand. She took his hand to shake and it disappeared into the great blackness of his own large hand. He remembered how later they had laughed when she had told him that on the day they had first met, how when she put her hand in his, that she had suddenly felt like a 7 year old girl shaking hands with an adult man, even though she was 5 years his senior. At the time, she did not know that Moses was that much younger than her, but it no longer mattered. She had fallen in love with the kindest soul that she would ever know. He, on the other hand, had loved Juliet from the day she arrived.

Moses had always looked up to her, despite her comparatively diminutive size. First, because he was still more child than man and she, a woman. Later, because it was clear to him that she was a natural leader where respect was an easy byproduct of their relationship. In the surrealism of today's activities, he stood like both a man and a child. The man loving her dearly and the child inside him frightened of the unknown. Juliet had always known what to do and he came to rely on her like a calf does it's mother. But more than anything, he had given his heart which was now teetering on the edge of a cliff that had no end to it's sinking depth.

The crowd of buyers and curiosity seekers gathered in the designated auction area conversing and laughing as if they were attending a social. The ancient Romans had festively gathered to watch gladiators inflict a gory death upon one another in times long past, so maybe it wasn't odd that man would still amuse himself at the suffering of those held in human bondage.

Moses was led to the back of the wagon like a man being led to the gallows. As he stood upon this hastily constructed stage of immorality, he searched his surroundings for any sight of Juliet.

In the distance, a wagon was heading south and he could make out a form sitting straight and proud. A red scarf was slowly disappearing as the wagon took a small hill and then descended to the other side. Moses called out her name in a wounded roar and as the red scarf disappeared from view, then forlornly whispering the name Juliet, over and over, while his body trembled and the cliff received his falling heart. No longer did he have a reason to live.

He would later lie down by the stream and allow those currents of time carry him to a better world.

It was now Harriet's turn to take her position on the wagon along with her newborn child in her arms. At least they would be sold together as the law required. All of John Russell Crafton's heirs were in attendance this day. Some counting their yet unreceived money. Some seeing their personal debts being wiped clean. Others there to buy. Their dissimilar needs similarly satisfied by the sale of human flesh.

When Harriet was being led up into the wagon, Newton Everhart shyly approached his mother, Mary Ann Russell Everhart, an heir to the estate and sister to Bennett, and spoke, "Mother. I worry about all the hard work you do around the farm and home. I think that buying Harriet and her child would relieve you of your burden around the home and farm, and especially as you become older."

Mothers know their children, more often than not, better than they know themselves, and Mary Ann quickly suspected that there was something more to her son's request than just concern for her well being. She saw deeply within Newton and detected that there was also concern for another. And maybe something more than just concern.

Newton was the same age as Harriet and they had known each other since childhood. Both were now 20 years old. Harriet was light skinned. A "mulatto". The child with her could easily pass as white. Tanned from the sun, but white. But what stood out on the child was the little girls grayish-blue eyes and hair that wasn't black, but actually a dark strawberry blond. *The same as her son.*

Mary Ann looked away from her son and stared at a physical world that had dissolved into a featureless landscape, and into the metaphysical world within herself. The bidding had begun. She sighed deeply and then stepped forward to enter into the bidding on Harriet. Mary Ann was the highest bidder and told Newton with a clipped shortness in her voice, "Get Harriet and the child and bring them to our wagon."

Mary Ann had looked forward to her share of the money. There was so much that she could have done with the money. Instead, her share of the estate proceeds had gone to the purchase of a young slave girl and her child that she herself had put up for auction. She suddenly and uncomfortably felt the imaginary weight of every eye pressing down on her and hurriedly walked away.

Harriet had been lucky, if in fact, a slave could ever be considered to be lucky. Her family had all been torn from her grasp, but the knowledge that she would remain near the man she loved, had already eased a pain that otherwise would have been unbearable.

One by one, until each of Juliet's family had been sold, the cries had become louder. The crowd of buyers and tag alongs never seemed to hear, except for those who had stood upon the back of a wagon to be sold like so much cattle at market. The list of names all told that fateful day shall be ever remembered:

Juliet
Moses
Harriet
Mary Jane
Amanda
Fanny
Rachael
Marshall
Granchison
Thomas
Wenny
Emily
Infant child of Amanda
Infant child of Mary Jane
Infant child of Harriet

Through the tears of time, their families have persisted and even flourished in the face of the great odds stacked against them. Their journey has been both long and often torturous but it is far from over.

James Bennett Everhart
Brother of John Newton Everhart
circa 1862

Chapter 35
War
1861

    Abolitionist in the North had been sounding the alarm for the past decade. If slavery was not abolished voluntarily, then force would be necessary. Nothing had given a better preview of the future than the firebrand from Kansas who had, only 2 years before, come to Virginia to incite a rebellion among the state's many slaves to fight for their freedom. He had passed through Clarke County, posing as a man who repaired clocks and using that opportunity to speak to the owner's slaves, encouraging them to rebel against their masters. John Brown's mission to have slaves rise up against their owners ended at a small federal arsenal in Harpers Ferry in the neighboring county of Jefferson. Brown has been captured, tried and sentenced to hang at the courthouse in Charles Town. The judge who presided over the trial was none other than Juliet's former attorney, *Richard E. Parker*. This one small incident had put the entire slave owning South on the defensive. It had not taken long before the South, fearing they would lose their slaves and therefore their wealth, to make the unprecedented move to secede from the United States and form their own government. That decision would result in the bloodiest war this country had ever seen before or since.

    The decision having been made for the South to secede from the Union, young men unaware of the horrors of war, eagerly, proudly and with great celebration, created and joined military units throughout every square mile of the South. Those who could afford the new uniforms of butternut or gray, strutted like minor gods throughout the streets of their hometowns, immortal and all powerful. Their youthful exuberance would soon enough fall to earth among the mortals.

   Clarke County formed several units of men, one infantry and one cavalry. Those who were able to own several horses and had the funds in which to care for their horses joined the cavalry. The Clarke Cavalry became Company D, 6th Virginia Cavalry led by the dashing and charismatic, Gen. J.E.B. Stuart.   All four of Bennett Russell's sons along with their Everhart cousins joined the Clarke Cavalry. Among the Everhart boys who joined, was John Newton Everhart. By war's end, Bennett would lose one son and another shot in the head at Brandy Station, left to die on the field, but recovered by Union forces where he eventually recovered with the bullet still lodged in his head. One of Newton Everhart's brothers, Jackson Everhart was killed in action at Brandy Station.

   The young slave girl, Harriet and Newton, the son of the woman who had purchased Harriet at the auction, had known each other since they were small children. The two had played together often, innocently unaware of their different colors or station in life. As they became young adults, their childhood relationship evolved into something more than mere friendship. Both were confused, frightened and torn with mixed emotions. They were reluctant to enter into the taboo world of mixed relationships and had for a while, avoided one another, attempting to put a physical and emotional distance between them. Their attempt to end something before it began, fell well short of their intended goals.

   In 1854, at the age of 17 years, Newton became the father of Harriet's little girl, Ella. Ella had been named for Newton's grandmother, Ella Everhart. A slave girl and the son of the woman who had bought her, had inevitably crossed a societal line of color, falling heart first into the abyss of forbidden love.

Harriet had been outside doing chores when she saw Newton ride up in his new Confederate uniform on his chestnut mare. At first she had been stunned and speechless at the sight of a uniform that stood for the continuation of slavery. Her stunned silence slowly smoldered until it ignited into a visible but self contained anger. Angry that he would have the temerity to defend the cause of slavery and angry that she might someday soon see his lifeless body returned home to be buried in the family graveyard, leaving both her and their children behind. She wanted to pummel him with her small fists yet conversely hold him tightly in her arms for what she feared could be the last time. As a slave involved in a relationship with a white man where his own family remained in suspect denial, she knew that this was not the time or place to show open emotions. So, she turned and walked away from him, hoping to find a moment of private solitude where she could seek improbable answers to nearly impossible questions. What she found was the crushing weight of sadness and a world full of contradictions and hypocrisy.

Upon Harriet walking away, the joy and pride that Newton felt as he rode up to the farm instantly vanished at Harriet's abrupt departure. His misplaced ego had suddenly turned to sadness and shame. Newton now felt crushed between two competing and agonizing choices with both bringing it's own particular variant of dishonor and shame. With Harriet he felt ashamed for donning a uniform that signified the continuation of slavery and dishonored their own personal relationship. With his friends and family the act of not joining the new Confederacy would bring shame to his family and personal dishonor to himself. He had created his own prison where escape from such now seemed to be an impossibility. He now lived in two worlds that were diametrically opposed to one another where the gravitational forces of each, threatened an unintended collision between the two. The world of love that had spanned the gulf between race and the world of martial honor that widened the divide between race. For Newton, choosing either world, would have been an act of cowardice in the face of the other. He had unfortunately succumbed to the youthful intoxication of mass nationalism for a new country and the false glory of warfare. Harriet had sobered him, but not before he had thoughtlessly chosen a misguided war over the forces of love. As a result of his reckless decision, he now proceeded down a road of endless emotional torment and into a world of bloody conflict.

_____

June 9, 1863 – Brandy Station

Through the early morning fog, the first sounds of gunfire were heard. General J.E.B. Stuart of the CSA had paraded his troops the day before, celebrating the Confederate victory at Chancellorsville and anticipated the drive northward that would bring the war to the doorstep of the Union at a small insignificant town in Pennsylvania called Gettysburg. At 4:30 am, Stuart was caught completely off guard by the 11,000 mounted Union troops bearing down on the sleeping rebel army. Much of the Confederate cavalry never had time to saddle their horses and hastily rode off to meet the intruders on bareback.

Newton, his two brothers and all four of his Russell cousins quickly mounted their horses and formed a line with the others of Co. D 6th Va. Cavalry. On command, they rode towards the gunfire at a controlled trot. There was no time to dismount and form an infantry line. Nearly 20,000 horse and riders clashed with pistols firing and sabers flashing in the first rays of the morning sun.

Smoke from artillery pieces trained on the rebel cavalry, mixed with the fog, created a chaotic scene of human and equine carnage. By noon, dead and dying horses, along with soldiers of both sides littered the field of battle. So much blood was spilled at such close quarters that it was impossible to tell whether the blood belonged to them or to their enemy.

The largest cavalry engagement ever seen on America's soil did not end until sunset the same day. For 14 hours each side had not so much fought to win, but fought to survive. As both armies withdrew in waning hours of the day, riderless horses wandered the field more often than not with their own wounds and many would surrender to pure exhaustion or to their own wounds, lying down alongside their human counterparts of war. As units reformed, they began to take stock of who had been left behind dying or dead.

Newton rode up to his brother James and shouted, "Have you seen Jack?"

Jack was his brother, Jackson Kennan Everhart.

James shouted back, "He was with us in the afternoon and then lost track of him. Cousin Tom's mare was found wandering the field with a bullet in her neck. She was led back by some of the boys and they are taking care of her, but we haven't seen Tom, neither!"

The end of this bloody engagement was still fresh and no one had time to reflect how or why they had come through this killing field alive. That would have to come later.

Both Newton and James turned their attention back toward the smoke and blood ridden battlefield knowing what they had to do next. "Let's go!" replied Newton, already wheeling his horse back towards the human and animal carnage.

The moans of wounded soldiers filled the night air. Newton thought that he would never be able to wash away the smell of death that soaked his jacket, pants and every pore on his body. After two hours of searching, they finally found Jack. He had been shot through his breast and a saber cut had opened a hideous gash down the length of his face that exposed jaw bone and teeth. Newton choked on his own vomit and tears as he cradled his brother in his arms, rocking softly back and forth like a small skiff in gentle waters.

Cousin Tom was never found. It was discovered later that he had been shot between the eyes and the Union Army, seeing that he was still barely alive, threw him on the back of a wagon with wounded and dead Yankees. Miraculously, Tom lived and was eventually paroled back home where his fighting days were over. He lived a full life and ironically married a woman whose father had operated an Underground Railroad for escaped slaves seeking their freedom. The aftermath of the war led to strange bedfellows, especially in the arena of love.

Tom Russell was reunited with his mare who had been shot through the neck at Brandy Station. It seemed like everyone in the area wanted to breed their stallion to his mare, just to have a foal from his famous old war horse. Tom would die exactly 20 years to the day after his mare succumbed to old age. He died in 1903.......with the bullet still lodged in his head.

   The war raged on for nearly two more years and in April 1865, Harriet, who had been on a far hill gathering firewood in twilight of the day, saw off into the distance, a lone rider dressed in drab brownish gray with what appeared to be a saber rattling by his side, turn towards the old toll road that led to the farm. She had been seeing a number of men returning from war the past week or two and had prayed that one might actually be Newton, safe and finally coming home. Each time she had been disappointed, but there was something about this particular horse and rider that captured a long ago familiar feeling. She began walking slowly down the hill with her eyes fixed upon the rider. She could now see that the hazy image was clearly a soldier. Unconsciously, she held her breath and then saw that this returning soldier was not riding past as all the others had, but was now guiding his horse onto the farm lane. Her slow, deliberate walk now turned into a mad dash that nearly sent her face first into a patch of early dandelions. Although the rider was slumped in apparent weariness and his clothing soiled, there was now no mistaking this rider. Newton had come home!

   As he swung himself from the saddle, he unbuckled his saber and let it drop unceremoniously forever from his side. All things war were no longer a part of his life. He no longer cared who was watching or what they would say. He had ridden for 3 hard days and at first he ran stiffly and slowly towards Harriet, but then as the effects of the harsh ride faded, he too ran faster and faster. His legs ran not from strength, but from love and desire. They met half way down the hill rushing into each others arms, holding onto each other like love struck entangled vines. Tears ran in rivers down each of their faces as they dropped to their knees as one unified entity and remained near motionless in the cool spring night, while the moon rose with it's soft light washing over them like a therapeutic cleansing. Newton would never be a coward in the world of love,…. *ever again.*

The world that they would now embark upon would have it's own challenges, and it's own dangers, but they would face them together until death do them part.

Chapter 36
From Swords to Plowshares

In 1867, Newton approached his cousin, Jesse Russell, a son of Bennett, who not only shared the same middle name of Newton, but had shared 4 years of riding into the waiting arms of death, battle after battle. They were only one year apart in age and had developed a bond that only war could queerly provide.

Newton was straight forward and stated, "Harriet is in need of her own place and needs land. Would you be willing to sell her several acres? Enough to build a home and grow enough crops to feed herself and her family."

Jesse was aware of his cousin's connection to Harriet, but it was never brought up. It would be no different now.

Jesse stated, "I have 3 acres in the corner of my farm I have little use for and believe I could sell Harriet that piece."

Greenville farm contained approximately 350 acres and was once part of the nearly 2,000 acres that that Jesse's father Bennett had owned and was part of Jesse's inheritance. The land had become fallow during the war and he needed money that the banks would no longer loan, in order to make the farm productive. He would have sold the land to Harriet anyway, and the prospect of money, no matter how small the amount, would be more than welcomed.

Newton asked, "How much for the land?"

"I figure $300 would be a fair price", replied Jesse.

Newton countered with, "We…..I mean, Harriet, only has $200."

Jesse smiled inwardly at Newt's near admission to their relationship.

They eventually settled on a price of $216. Harriet had more than $200 but there was no reason to let Jesse know that. She needed the extra money to build a small 2 room frame home and to purchase the necessities of housekeeping, not to mention the seeds needed to grow her garden.

Jesse suspected that Harriet had more money than his cousin had stated, but he had no desire to try to gouge more money out of Harriet. The war was over and people, *all people,* needed help. He also knew that Harriet was *family.* It remained unspoken, but family nevertheless. Families would not turn their backs on relatives in need if there was anyway that one could help the other. It had been like that since the beginning of time.

Four years later, in 1871, Harriet would purchase a ¼ acre lot in Berryville for slightly over $250.

She sold her 3 acre lot the same year for $400. She may not have known how to read or write, but she certainly knew the art of the deal. The land in Berryville had formerly belonged to George W. Diffenderfer, husband of Newton's sister Rebecca Everhart. Harriet understood both the financial value of owning land, but even more importantly, the value it contributed to one's own self worth as a person. As far as Harriet knew, she was the first in her family to become a land owner. Nothing could have put more distance between being a slave and that of being a freed person, than land ownership. She only wished that her mother, Juliet, could be there with her to share the dream that began with her mother so many years before. Harriet would name one of her children in honor of her mother, thus keeping Juliet's indomitable spirit alive within the hearts and minds of future generations.

Chapter 37
Reconstruction and Jim Crow

For most Southern men, the end of the war ushered in the beginning of an era that denied any man who supported the Confederacy, which was nearly all, the right to vote or hold office. The destructive nature of the war had resulted in the destitution of the South and Reconstruction, meant to compassionately rebuild a war torn nation, had transformed to a punishment of those who had dared rebel against the sovereignty of the Union. This was not the intention of President Lincoln, but an assassin's bullet had, whether the South knew it or not, ended their best hope for the future. The occupying Union Army found it amusing to see their former enemies struggle to eke out a living, but found it even more amusing to give former slaves more status than their former owners. What they didn't know, was that they were adding fuel to the fire of new form of violent racism that would plague the South for decades to come and continues to exist in both more subtle, and overt ways, to this very day. Although, the hatred of the black man was more intense in the deep South, Clarke County certainly had their issues as well. For Newton and Harriet the dangers of war had ended, but they were now caught in the crossfire of a different sort that was equally as dangerous, and at times, equally horrific. They would live in a world that belonged to neither of them and both would walk within the ghostly shadows of the past that would lengthen into the present and beyond.

The era of Reconstruction would last until 1877, only to be replaced by the degrading, disenfranchising and prejudicial laws of the Jim Crow era. These laws that humiliated an entire race of people remained for over three-fourths of a century. Harriet ensured that her children could read and write and this may have been her wisest investment of all. Old Jim Crow could try to keep her family pseudo-enslaved, but she knew, just like her mother, it could not enslave the mind, unless you allowed it to. Harriet had no intention of allowing enslavement, regardless of what form it took.

By 1877, all knew that Newton and Harriet were living together openly on the western edge of Berryville. Newton was still part of the family farm some 3 miles away from Berryville and rode his old war horse, now in her early 20's, out to the farm every day. Each evening he would remount the horse that had carried him safely through the war back to the peace and joy that was Harriet.

The law prevented blacks and whites from marrying, but looked the other way when a mixed couple chose to live together that reflected much of the peculiar and contradictory ways of the South. So, Harriet and Newton spent their lives as lawfully unrecognized man and wife under the disapproving eyes of the community.

Growing up, Newton never gave much thought to the word nigger. It was used so often that he had just accepted it's usage. This was all about to change for him in a sudden rush of a life altering awareness.

Like his brothers, he was tall and stood 6 feet in height. Like his brothers, he had experienced the violence and bloodshed of war. And like his brothers, if pushed to fight, he did so without fear or thought. Survival in war has a way of making one no longer fear death at the hands of another. They all assumed that if they had survived the bloodiest battles fought during the Civil War, then they may indeed be immortal. These men were dangerous when crossed, ...*or if family was crossed*.

The days of summer had been oppressively hot and humid. Tempers were as short as the days were long. Men who were naturally mean, were especially so in the unceasing heat wave. To add insult to injury, what was known as the Panic of 1873 had brought on an economic depression that would not end until 1879. Banks had failed and those that didn't, were miserly with the little money they did have to loan. Farms were going under and jobs were scarce. The jobless men wandered the streets of Berryville daily, disillusioned, angry and often, drunk. It was on one of these days that Newton awoke to the fact that the word "nigger" took on a whole new meaning. It was no longer just idle talk by idle men, but became a word that made him cringe whenever he heard this demeaning term. Today, it went beyond cringing. Today he understood the hurt.......and the anger this hateful word could produce in oneself.

Newton had just returned to Harriet's home and she was sitting on the front porch hoping for a stray breeze and fanning herself in hope of temporary relief from the unyielding heat when he heard that inflammatory word that would from that day forward, forever make his blood run cold.

"You should be used to this heat, *nigger woman*! It ain't like you and all them other niggers weren't use to it over in Africa long before y'all got here! And that is exactly where you niggers need to go. Over in Africa with a god damn spear and not out on some fancy porch fanning yourself like some queen of the jungle!" shouted a drunken ruffian from the street.

Newton turned to the man and said, "You owe this woman an apology. NOW!"

The man was far shorter than Newton, but the cheap liquor he had greedily consumed earlier had given him the false and later, regrettable courage to continue his ill advised slurs.

"And what you gonna do about it.........*nigger lover!*"

Newton never replied. It was never about what the man had called him. He had heard this said to him before. Even though that term disparaged both Harriet and himself, he had kept himself in check, always walking away not wanting to create more problems than they both already endured. But, this was the first time that he had witnessed someone calling Harriet a *nigger*, and this was not something he would walk away from. He walked quickly over to the man, grabbed him by his soiled and greasy collar and lifted him into the muggy Virginia air and began running with his wide eyed captive towards a tree, slamming him against it so hard that several walnuts were jarred loose from their branches.

With the man still dazed and in shock from his plastering against the old walnut tree, Newton threw him to the ground with such force that the man actually appeared to bounce before settling ignominiously in a helpless heap. Before the man could gather his wits about him, Newton began kicking the man in his ribs, his head, legs, and whatever part of the man Newton's booted feet could find. In between the groans, the man pleaded for Newton to stop. Newton no longer appeared capable of hearing. His eyes were glazed over in rage while he continued to kick the man until both of the man's eyes had swollen shut. Blood leaked, and then streamed out of his nose and mouth. Newton would have killed this man had he not somehow felt Harriet's caring but firm grip on his arm. He turned to her not quite recognizing who she was as first. Fury had taken over his body and his mind. He continued to look quizzically at her for several seconds until his senses slowly returned. She calmly took his hand and led him into the house like a mother would a small child.

From Harriet's window, she could see a man that had come so near to death, drag himself away from the scene of his brutal beating. Using Newton's horse to pull himself up, the old war horse danced sideways and craned her neck back towards this unfamiliar intruder. Her lips were curled and her eyes and nose flared as her teeth clamped on the upper arm of her unsuspecting victim.

The former war horse had used her teeth a number of times when crowded against the enemy's steeds during close quarter engagements. It was not unusual for horses to develop this self preservation fighting tactic that was reminiscent of a time when horses roamed wild and fought to survive. Unfortunately, many horses would be shot out from under their rider before their ancient self preservation skills could develop. It also wasn't unusual to see men training their new and untested horses to engage the enemy's horse in this fashion.

Warriors had been training their horses in the crude art of warfare since at least the Crusades, when Knights Templar's had made it part of their war horse's training. By inflicting pain in the other horse, their equine enemy would always respond with a violent avoidance reaction. Such sudden and unexpected movement of the horse could either help to unseat it's rider or at the very least, change the angle of a swords intended blow, potentially saving the knight's life and putting the enemy in a vulnerable position that would allow for his own killing blow. Not only were these large war horses trained to bite, but also to wheel and kick with nothing more than a slight pressure of the rider's leg. A well placed kick could break the ribs of another horse or kill an infantryman on foot. Newton's horse had been trained in the same manner of these old knights of lore had trained their horses.

This drunken, and now thoroughly beaten man, screamed out in pain as Newton's horse viciously clamped on his upper arm. The mare then tossed her head with equally vicious force sending the man flying through the air with the ease on one throwing out the garbage from an upstairs window. The horse now wheeled to kick. It was only a glancing blow, but enough to break his arm. The sickening snap of the bone could be heard from inside the house. He would never have proper range of his shoulder and arm ever again. He would never walk by Harriet's home again and…. he would also never walk closer than 10 feet from a horse that he himself didn't own.

Newton had come to the window with Harriet and saw what his mare had done. He smiled and said, "I'll miss that horse when she goes."

Harriet took her eyes away from the window and looked questionably at Newton. Pausing for a moment, she suddenly let out a laugh, while shaking her head in mock disbelief.

After her tension breaking laugh, she teasingly asked Newton, "What are you making us for dinner?"

It was his turn to laugh. The last time he had tried making dinner, it was unrecognizable and Harriet had thrown it out for a stray dog that had suspiciously sniffed at it, and then continued on his way. Newton was never again allowed in the kitchen. The stray dog was never seen around their house again.

Harriet and Newton spent their entire lives together that had begin in the antebellum South and carried through the Civil War, Reconstruction Era, Jim Crow South, the Spanish American War and WW I. As they aged they found a peace that only time can provide to those who had endured more than their fair share of hardships from a world that was often angry, prejudiced and too often laden without compassion.

Raising 9 children who were neither white nor black, she understood more keenly than most the necessity of educating her children. Only through education, would her children have any chance of leaving behind the old decaying fields of former plantations and move beyond a past of human bondage, and into a future with hope and possibility.

Several small one room schools for blacks had begun to spring up throughout the county during Reconstruction and Harriet and Newton made sure that each would attend one of these schools, regardless of the miles of walking it would take to travel to the nearest little school. Their children were not excused because of snow, no matter the amount that had fallen. When the snow had gotten too deep for the littlest of them to walk through, the older children would put them on their backs and carry them. Missing school was not an option in the Phillips household. Although the teacher had little patience with those who chose to skip school and was a strict disciplinarian, nothing the teacher did could compare to what Harriet would do if they were caught not attending classes. Kind and loving in every other way with her children, she would not tolerate their willful disrespect of learning. Education was not an option for her when growing up and *not* taking advantage of education was *not* an option she gave her children.

When her children grew into adulthood, their memories would often carry them back to those childhood days with both fondness and gratitude for Harriet's unfailing and uncompromising belief in education. Each would pass the need for education onto the next generation.

All through Harriet's children's lives, she would push them to reach greater heights. Whenever they complained of being unable to do something without even attempting the task at hand, Harriet would inevitably end her scolding with *"If you don't' jump in the pond, you nevuh gonna swim."*

When they became adults with children of their own, those same words were echoed to the next generation and the next generation after that. These simple words first uttered by Juliet, would be said a thousand times be each following generation and even spread to other families of the African American community. Failure is a part of everyone's life, but failure as a result of not first trying could not, in Harriet's eyes, be forgiven. She made it her 11th commandment, giving it the same degree of sin as the first Ten commandments. When failures did occur, their was no shame if one had first given their best. One could not ask more of a person. The shame was in not trying.

Chapter 38
The Death of Newton

In 1917, the U.S. entered into WWI, bringing with it, not only the deaths of the young Clarke County boys who died in this brutal form of trench warfare, but also the greatest pandemic flu the world had ever experienced. It would be known as the Spanish flu, which infected 500 million people worldwide and would result in death for nearly 100 million of them. The first case and death of this flu in the U.S. occurred January 1918 and would spread with unforgiving speed across the country. In early May of 1918, the then 81 year old Newton Everhart developed a fever. The Spanish flu had made it's deadly arrival to Clarke County.

Newton continued to fail, and as he weakened, he began to succumb to life's final gasp. Pneumonia was the Spanish Flu's terminal blow and Newton received it with stoic resignation. His time on this earth was coming to an end, when suddenly a knock on Harriet's door jarred her from her prayers.

Harriet, still a spry woman at age 83, opened the door, and standing there were two members of Newton's family. Newton's family seldom came to her house, and when they did, it was never for a friendly conversational visit. Today was no different, although the reason for their unexpected visit today could not have been more different. The emotional scarring that Harriet would endure from this final visit by Newton's family would not be limited to just herself, but would be passed sadly onto future generations as well.

With stern faces, the oldest of the two Everhart men bluntly stated, "We're here to take uncle Newton back home."

Harriet replied, "He's already home."

"I don't think you understand, *Miss Phillips.* Uncle Newton is dying and we won't have him die in a….. *Negro woman's* house."

Harriet never hesitated and replied, "But I guess it was alright that I *cooked for him, sewed his clothes, cleaned house for him, shared my bed with him,* and done so for the past 50 years, but somehow I ain't good enough to comfort him in his last days!? That seem about right, to y'all?"

Her unwanted visitors stood stunned for a moment and then said, "We ain't here to ask you permission. You best step aside *Miss Phillips.* We're taking uncle Newt back with us whether you like it or not!"

They then brushed past Harriet as if she was nothing more than an inanimate object and entered the small bedroom to quickly remove their sickly uncle with a haste normally reserved for the rescuing of a child from a burning fire.

As they reached down to carry their uncle out, his eyelids hung like an old pair of curtains cut too short for their unwashed windows, allowing a minimal, and distorted view of the world beyond it's walls. Age and sickness had left his mind immersed in a low lying fog that randomly thinned and thickened, providing brief moments of a fractured visibility of his shrinking world.

Through the haze of his illness, a cloudy window in his mind briefly opened, allowing him to understand who they were, and what they were preparing to do.

He weakly, yet defiantly, croaked, "Leave me be, boys! I'm dying and I plan to die here where I have spent the better part of my days on this here earth. Harriet is my wife ….*even though the damn law don't abide by it*! The law, them who wrote it, as well as you boys, can go to **hell**!"

His short tirade had drained his last drop of energy and he involuntarily sank back into a fitful silence.

He was far to weak to put up any kind of fight, and as they carried him out to the wagon, he made moaning noises, not so much from the pain of being roughly lifted from the comfort of his bed, but from the pain it inflicted deep within his tortured heart.

As the wagon bumped along the road, Newton reached his hand into his front pocket and with bent and stiff fingers, he found what he was looking for and clasped his hand around it. He had touched that old coin for over 60 years and with this last touch, over 60 years of memories infused him with the warmth of love….and the person who made it so.

When the wagon that carried Newton disappeared from sight, Harriet reached into her pocket and pulled out an old tarnished coin with a symbol imprinted on it showing two hands clasped together. The same coin that she had found so many years before when she and Newton sat beside the old pond at Rock Hall. Her eyes filled with tears while her fingers gently caressed the old coin. No longer able to stand, she sat with her face in her hands filling them with a flood of tearful memories.

Two days later on May 16, 1918, John Newton Everhart passed away. He was buried quietly and with little ceremony at the cemetery in Berryville, known as Green Hill. He had no pall bearers and no family or friends attending that day. None of the men he had faithfully served with throughout the hardships and camaraderie of war for 4 long years showed up to give their last respects. He had only the grave digger to watch over him as he was lowered into the ground,…. save one solitary figure dressed in black standing at the stone walled entrance of the burial grounds. The one person who had come to give their last respects was prohibited from entering……. due to nothing more than just her color. There would be no room for Harriet in a cemetery that did not welcome *her type*. Either in life or in death.

Harriet would live another 10 years and see her 9 children grow up and have children of their own. As she had done with each of her infant children, she also did with her infant grandchildren and great grandchildren. Using both hands, she lovingly explored every part of their bodies, always amazed with the miracle of life, and seemingly imparting to each child with just her touch, the imprint of the lives of all those that came before.

On an early spring day, the former Miss Eliza Tucker Carter, now the wife of Harriet's son, Henry Hampton Phillips, arrived at Harriet's door with a small bundle in her arms. Careful to knock on the door for fear of dropping her bundle, Harriet opened the door and her eyes and smile both widened at what she saw.

Harriet, bringing her hand over her heart said, "Lordy! What a beautiful baby! And what to you call
this little bundle of joy?"

Eliza smiled and softly said, "Ella. Ella Nora Phillips."

Harriet reached her hands out toward the newborn where Eliza carefully handed Ella over to her. As she did with all her newborn family, she moved her hands gently over the child, but unlike the others, Harriet seemed to have entered a trance, and prolonging her exploration of Ella's small body.

After several minutes, Harriet opened her eyes and looked at Eliza, saying, "All children are special, Liza, but I sense something more here. This child gonna do great things. Mark my words! The Lord done sent you a gift. More than the gift of life itself, but sumpin' more special than you know."

Special she was.

Chapter 39
The Death of Harriet

On June 29, 1928 at 88 years of age, Harriet passed into the hands of her Lord. Ella's phone at her and Bill's drugstore rang that day with the news of Harriet's passing.

Harriet slowly hung up the phone, her vision now clouded by the onset of tears and said to her husband Bill, "Harriet's gone. I'll be taking the train back to Virginia as soon as the next one leaves. Will you be alright here to run the store until I get back?"

Bill walked over and put her arms around Ella, feeling her body now beginning to heave with her choking sobs. After Ella had gotten through the worst of the initial shock of losing Harriet, Bill said, "You go for as long as you need. I'll be fine here."

With a hand laid softly on Bill's cheek, Ella replied, "I know you will be. She was old, you know. But I never wanted to consider the eventuality of her death. We just put these things out of the front of our minds and tuck them safely away in some quiet spot hoping that if you never think about someone dying, that they will continue to live forever." Tears once again began to trickle down Ella's face.

Bill, "She will live forever. She lives through you. She lives through her children, her grandchildren and God willing, she will live in the hearts of each future generation."

Ella replied, "And this is just one of the reasons I love you so, Bill. You always know the right thing to say. Some may look at my strength and think it all comes from me. What they don't realize is that strength is only as good as those you choose to surround yourself with, and I have chosen the very best in having chosen you."

Chapter 40
The Wake

Twilight had arrived along with the train carrying Ella into the Berryville train depot. Little in this sleepy southern town had changed since she had left 12 years earlier. She could almost swear that the same old cat was still lying on the train master's window counter and that the same passengers waiting for the arrival of their train had been patiently waiting for the past dozen years. Ella had visited her old hometown several times over the years, but now wished she had done so far more often. Harriet was gone and she hadn't been able to say goodbye the way she would have liked. With an onslaught of regret and partial resignation, Ella thought to herself, *we so seldom do.*

Ella had taken a seat outdoors under the depot's canopied roof and could feel the disapproving eyes of the smattering of folks at the station. She apparently had the *temerity* to have dressed better than most of the white folks at the station. Now that she was successful, what was she to do? Dress like a field hand just to give them comfort in their own prejudice? No doubt that they would resolve their discomfort by emphatically using the term, *uppity.* Yes. Berryville, and the country in general, had changed little over these past 12 years.

As Ella turned away from this pervasive ignorance, she saw a wagon turning onto the depot road and immediately recognized two of her brothers. Walker and Bowles bounced along the pot holed road waving their arms at Ella. Walker was 3 years younger than Ella and Bowles had been the youngest of the siblings but was now on the cusp of adulthood. The last time Ella had seen Bowles, he was only 12 years old. Both of her brothers would be described as stout, but Walker was a tall man, where Bowles was of average height, although his stocky frame made him appear shorter than he actually was.

When the wagon pulled up, Walker leaped from the buckboard to warmly greet his older sister. Bowles shyly remained in the wagon, not sure if Ella remembered him or how he should greet someone he had barely known during his lifetime, especially someone who had been given a kind of celebrity status by family members. He needn't have worried.

After Ella and Walker had embraced, she turned to Bowles, "Is that anyway to greet your sister, *Bowles*?"

A large smile creased Bowles' face, obviously relieved and happy that Ella had remembered him.

"I ain't forgotten you, Ella!" shouted Bowles

Ella, *"Haven't."*

Bowles answered confusingly, *"Haven't* what?"

Ella replied, "I *haven't* forgotten you.

Stuttering, Bowles replied, "um, er, yes mam. I meant to say, *haven't* forgotten you."

Ella and Walker both laughed and Ella said, "Get down here boy and give me a hug."

Bowles cheerfully did as instructed. Any grammatical embarrassment he may have felt just moments before was quickly replaced by starry eyed admiration and love for his sister.

The wagon only had room for two on the buckboard, so Bowles perched himself on the back of the wagon with his legs dangling over the side.

Once all were settled in the wagon, Walker said, "All of the family is here and they sure are going to be happy to see you. Right now, they could use a little happiness! Miss Harriet will be sorely missed." Pausing for a moment, Walker continued, "You two were mighty close. How you holdin' up, Ella?"

Sadness veiled Ella's face and she couldn't help to look away before answering, "Been better days....better days." Walker silently nodded his head. The ride up to their grandmother's home was silent except for the distant staccato calling of locusts announcing summer's humid arrival and the mournful call of a solitary dove. These were the sounds of Ella's youth and they would forever be a part of her, although today, these sounds of her youthful carefree days, only seemed to intensify her silent grieving for Harriet.

After a busy day preparing for Harriet's wake, the time had finally arrived for family and friends to gather at the small white church with it's distinctive green bell tower topped with a simple cross. It took a dozen wagons provided and driven by the many friends of Harriet to carry the family to the church in solemn progression. Most of the town had heard about Harriet's death and as they passed people on the streets, many men doffed their caps in honest respect. Even many white men stood with hat in hand. Ella couldn't help but think that dying seemed to be an extreme way to finally receive that which had escaped so many in life. *Respect.* Respect, regardless of color. It was at this exact moment that Ella knew what she was truly meant to do on God's green earth. Change perceptions, tear down the barriers of Jim Crow laws, and build for a future. But it would take more than just her. It would take a community. A countrywide community. She was ready to do her part. But for now, there was a more pressing matter.

The church was filled with friends and family dressed in their Sunday best. As was tradition, the casket was open to view. One by one, each filed by Harriet's casket to look upon her for the last time. Harriet seemed smaller than she had in life and one couldn't be sure if in some ways, she had only been seen as larger, due to her strength and respect in her community and not to actual physical stature.

Ella had stood in the rear of the church receiving friends and family. The congregation had been drawn to Ella and it was clear that the baton had been passed on to her but she knew that her time in Berryville was over and had been for sometime now. She could not be her grandmother, but she could take what Harriet had given her and pass it on to a whole new generation that would not be limited to just her own family, but to a much larger family. If the Negro race was to succeed, then they must unite as one extended family that shared the same struggles from coast to coast. Ella had been given a gift and to not use it to help others would have been a sin in her mind. The journey would be arduous, and she knew that she might not be able finish the journey, but the start of the path was clear and she was certain that there would always be another to accept the baton and continue the journey to the finish line.

As Ella stood, warmly accepting heartfelt condolences, the normal hushed tones of those gathered at the church were occasionally interrupted by the wail of a woman's voice as they took their turn in front of Harriet's casket. Softer crying was heard among those who sat in the hard straight back wooden pews. It was finally time for Ella to say her last goodbye to Harriet, so she excused herself from the throng of people around her and made her way to the casket.

Ella felt as if her legs were turning to melted butter, but she also knew that she must remain strong. Not only for the family, but for Harriet as well. Harriet would have expected no less from her. As Ella gazed down on Harriet, she suddenly experienced a calm enveloping here. It was the same calm she would experience as a little girl who came to Harriet crying when she had hurt herself or had awoken from a nightmare. Harriet would then hold her tightly in her arms until Ella's pain or fear passed. When Ella's little girl had died, she found herself having doubts about God's benevolence, but now, standing before the woman she loved, God seemed to have merged with Harriet to bring Ella a much desired peace of mind and spirit.

Ella was dressed in a simple black linen dress and large brimmed matching hat. In her hand she carried a large handbag from which she removed what appeared to be a loosely rolled paper approximately 14 inches from top to bottom of the paper cylinder. It was secured with a red ribbon around it's middle tied with a neat bow. She then gently placed it in Harriet's hands which had been crossed over her breast in the typical pose of death. A minute and barely visible stamp mark showed on one corner of the paper, that on closer inspection, read, *"University of Pittsburgh."*

Ella then spoke in a whisper reciting the words she had heard a thousand times over, *"If you don't jump in the pond, you ain't nevuh gonna swim."* Ella then stood fully erect and softly, yet firmly, said, "I learned to swim Miss Harriet, and it was you who really earned this diploma."

As the family rode from the church that evening they all were transfixed on the setting sun. Never had any seen such a bold color in the sky. The western sky appeared to have been draped with a scarf of bright red resting upon the low darkness of the night to come.

No one had said a word on the ride home until Ella quietly spoke, "Juliet."

Her brother Walker who was guiding the horse drawn wagon home turned to her and questioned,"What, did you say?"

Ella answered, "An old memory suddenly came back to me. Something Miss Harriet had told me as a little girl. Miss Harriet didn't spend much time telling stories from the days when she and her family were slaves. It is a dark period of time that our people wish to put behind them. The wounds have not yet fully healed, and to pick at that wound would have only allowed it to fester in their hearts. But, Miss Harriet did mention her mother from time to time but it was difficult for her. You see... Juliet, Miss Harriet, and all their family were sold at slave auction and Juliet….. she was never heard from again. Miss Harriet carried much pain and sorrow inside. Hidden deep within her.

Walker getting a little agitated by Ella's answer, pushed forward, "So, what was the story Miss Harriet told you?"

Ella, hearing the impatience in Walker's voice, patted him on the leg and replied, "Miss Harriet told me that Juliet always wore a beautiful bright red scarf tied around her head. This evening's sky reminded me of a red scarf and that reminded me of what Miss Harriet had told me about Juliet. Maybe this is Juliet's way of telling us that she is here...and always will be."

The wagon carrying Walker and Ella rolled to a stop in front of Harriet's home. Neither made an attempt to climb out of the wagon, but sat wordlessly with their eyes turned skyward in the sublime wonderment of something far greater than themselves. As the light faded, a warm breeze brushed their faces and just as quickly as the breeze arose, it seemed to lift skyward, passing into the night.

Author's Note

As previously mentioned in the Foreword, the characters were actual people with just several exceptions. The trial, the outcome, the ensuing slave auction, Newton's brother Jackson killed at Brandy Station, as well as Tom Russell shot between the eyes, Harriet and Newton's life together, and the circumstances of Newton's death are all actual events. The personalities I created for the characters, although fictional, were nevertheless based on what we know of the people from this time period with the author attempting to bring the characters to life in a way that not only depicts the world of slave and slave owner and the world they lived in, but also to show that human nature, no matter the time period in our history, remains very much the same. Love, anger, power, money, and struggles for a better life have been, and always will be, part of the human story. The following will help the reader separate fact from fiction:

Bennett Russell and Others vs. Negroes Juliet and Others – This was an actual court case that took place from 1848 to 1856. It began in Clarke County, Virginia and was transferred to Winchester, Virginia in 1851 when Juliet's attorney was appointed to the 13th Circuit Court for Clarke and Jefferson Counties after the sudden death of Judge Douglas. The suit was brought against Juliet by Bennett Russell and his siblings when Juliet's attorney recorded the original will of John Russell Crafton dated 1839, which had provided for the freedom of his slaves. Shortly after the original will was recorded after Crafton's death in 1848, Bennett Russell and his siblings recorded a document dated 1842 that became known as the Articles of Agreement which had in effect revoked the slave's freedom and directed that they all be sold and the money raised from the sale be divided between the heirs.

Articles of Agreement – As previously stated, the Articles of Agreement revoked the slaves freedom and directed that the slaves be sold. It was written 3 years after the original will. It was witnessed by Bennett Russell, Thomas W. Russell, John Russell (eldest son of Bennett) and a man named William R. Spurr. Manumission clauses in wills too often were challenged by the deceased heirs through myriad ways of legal maneuvering and juries made up of sympathetic slave owners. An expert in wills and suits regarding manumission found a number of suspect parts of the Articles that was familiar to her and helped point these out to me which I included in the story itself.

The Slave Auction in 1856 – The auction did take place and Juliet and Marshall were the first to be sold. Bennett Russell's sister, Mary Ann Russell Everhart did purchase Harriet, an infant child and a small girl named Ellen. John Newton Everhart was her son and spent his life with Harriet. He fathered all 9 of Harriet's children.

John Russell Crafton – Born in 1772, all that is known about him is that his mother's maiden name was Russell and most likely from the King William County area of Virginia, where his father, Major Bennett Crafton was born and spent much of his life until 1776 where he left for Granville, North Carolina and joined the 6th NC Militia. First records of John Russell Crafton coming to the Frederick and Clarke County area of Virginia was in the early 1790s according to tax records. He married in 1799 to Ann Wason in Winchester, Virginia. What we can tell from tax records is that in all likelihood he owned a teamster business. He wrote his will in 1839 and died in 1848. He named all the slaves in his will. They were named again, along with their ages, in 1850 in the estate accounting records for John Russell Crafton.

Bennett Russell – Born in 1799, he was the eldest son of John Russell Crafton. He was appointed administrator of the estate of his father by the court. The original will of 1839 did not appoint an executor of the estate. Bennett did own 1,908 acres at the time of his death in 1862. He was elected as a Gentleman Justice to the courts of Clarke County in 1856. He did murder a man named Burr E. Barr and found not guilty as a result of self defense in 1860. In the story, I give this an earlier date in order for the reader to have a better feel for Bennett Russell.

Bennett Crafton – Born in the 1730s in King William County, he was in the import/export business, read law and was a certified surveyor. He left King William in 1776 and joined the 6th NC Militia at Granville, North Carolina and made the Adjutant with the rank of Major. Her served in the war in both Pennsylvania, North Carolina and mainly in South Carolina until the end of the Revolutionary War in 1783. His son was John Russell Crafton. John Russell Crafton dropped the Crafton surname and the family went by the surname Russell ever since. Bennett Crafton lived in Edgefield County, SC after the war and died on a business trip to Charleston, SC in 1785. He left his entire estate to a much younger brother named Samuel Crafton leaving both John Russell Crafton and another son named Richard out of the will.

Richard E. Parker, Jr. – Born 1810 and died 1893. His father, Col. Richard E. Parker, Sr., had built Soldier's Retreat (The Retreat) snuggled between the Shenandoah River and the Blue Ridge. He was a prominent farmer, lawyer and judge. Richard E. Parker, Jr. was also a prominent farmer, lawyer and later elected judge in 1851 to the 13th Circuit Court District after the death of Judge Douglas. He was the presiding judge in the trial of abolitionist John Brown at a court held in Jefferson County in 1859.

Judge Issac R. Douglas – Born 1790 in Jefferson County, WV

(formerly Virginia) and died May 28, 1851. He lived on the edge
of Charles Town at his home he called "Mordington". It was
formerly owned by Charles Washington, youngest brother to
George Washington. The original name of the home was "Happy
Retreat." He presided over the trial of Juliet until his death in
1851. Due to the appointment of Richard E. Parker, Jr. as judge
of the same district, the trial was moved to Winchester, Frederick
County, Virginia.

Briggs Family – The Briggs family moved to Clarke County
from Stafford County, Virginia. Their descendant did own an
import/export business and was approximately the same age as
Bennett Crafton who was engaged in the same business in King
William County. There is good reason to believe that the
relationship between the Clarke Co. Briggs family and John
Russell Crafton was based on business relationships between the
two families from a generation before. Thomas Briggs and his
two sons, Thomas and William, did witness the will of John
Russell Crafton.

William R. Spurr – Little is known of Spurr other than his
occupation was a "saddler" and had witnessed the signing of the
Articles of Agreement. During the trial he was living in the far
western hills of Virginia (now West Virginia). It was agreed that
he could send in his testimony as to the witnessing of the Articles.
There was a young man that very well could have been his son,
named William Spurr who was convicted of murder in Clarke
County in 1859. He was sent to prison in Richmond but released
with all other prisoners there at the beginning of the Civil War.

Thomas W. Russell - Born 1812 and died 1898. Was the brother of Bennett Russell and signed the Articles of Agreement as a witness. He had been engaged in several failed and successful business ventures.

John Wm Russell – Born 1827 and died 1898. Was the eldest son of Bennett Russell. He inherited the farm known as North End where he built a large stone home that was later destroyed by fire in the early 1960s. He was the last person buried at the old family graveyard on the farm. He signed the Articles of Agreement as a witness.

Peter Cain – He had hired Marshall in 1853 when Marshall attempted to flee to freedom. This family lived on Senseny Road approximately 4 miles from Bennett Russell's farm. There was an old frame church on his property known as Cain's Chapel. It fell into disrepair after the civil war and by the 1870s the little chapel disappeared altogether. An old graveyard remains next to where the chapel once stood. His depiction as a part time minister at the Cain's Chapel is pure fiction.

Philip Williams – Born 1802 and died 1868 of a stroke during a trial. Williams was born in Shenandoah County, Virginia, studied law and admitted to the bar in the 1820s where he moved to Winchester to practice law. He was the attorney for Bennett Russell.

Robert Young Conrad – Born 1805 and died 1875. Conrad had first entered the U.S. Military Academy (West Point), but left to study law. He took over representing Juliet in 1851 when Parker was appointed as the judge to the 13th Circuit Court District. He lived in Winchester, Virginia.

Mary Ann Russell Everhart – Born 1801 and died 1865. She was the sister of Bennett Russell and one of the heirs of John Russell

Crafton. In 1856, she purchased her daughter in law, Harriet and two of her grandchildren at the slave auction in 1856. Her son, John Newton Everhart, lived his entire life with Harriet and fathered 9 children with her.

John Newton Everhart – Born 1837 and died 1918. John Newton Everhart was known as "Newton" and was the husband (although not recognized by Virginia) of Harriet. He did join the Clarke Cavalry, Co. D, 6th Virginia Cavalry along with several brothers and the sons of Bennett Russell. While on his death bed at Harriet's and his home in Berryville, family members came and removed him to take him "home." According to Harriet Phillips' descendants, he was removed from his home so that he would not die in "a negro woman's home."

Jackson K. Everhart – Born 1842 and died 1863. Jackson was the brother of Newton Everhart and did join the Clarke Cavalry, was captured in Millwood, Virginia in early April 1863 and shortly thereafter paroled in latter April, 1863. He fought in the Battle of Brandy Station June 9, 1863 where he was killed in action.

Thomas J. Russell – Born 1840 and died 1903. Thomas J. was the son of Bennett Russell and also served with the Clarke Cavalry. He participated in the Battle of Brandy Station and was shot between the eyes and left for dead. Union troops nursed him back to health and he was later paroled home. His mare was shot through the neck at the same battle, rescued by the men of the Clarke Cavalry and nursed back to health and produced a number of much sought after foals. Thomas J. did marry a woman by the name of Elizabeth Mary Simpers in Fauquier County whose family had run an underground railroad helping escaped slaves make their way north to freedom.

Jesse Newton Russell – Born 1838 and died 1903. Jesse also served in the Clarke Cavalry. He inherited a farm known as Greenville from his father, Bennett Russell. Harriet had purchased 3 acres from a family named Carter from land that had been subdivided off Greenville. Harriet's sister, Amanda, who had been purchased at the auction by another sister of Bennett Russell, also purchased several acres from Jesse Newton Russell and for a time, lived next door to Harriet Phillips.

Col. James Castleman – A prominent citizen of Clarke County who lived at North Hill on the opposite side of the Shenandoah River from Richard E. Parker. He operated a ferry, tavern and farm. The death of the slave Lewis was widely reported in newspapers. The Washington paper *National Era* reported on the murder trial November 6, 1851 with vivid detail of the events. Harriet Beecher Stowe also wrote about it in her book, *Tale of the Great Dismal Swamp, Vol. II* in 1856. She had stated that she also used the horror of Lewis' murder in arguably the most well known book of all time in this country, *Uncle Tom's Cabin.* Castleman died in 1854. The crossing at the Shenandoah River is still known today as Castleman's Ferry.

 Clarke Cavalry – The 6th Virginia Cavalry fought in nearly every major battle during the Civil War, including Gettysburg. Co. D was made up primarily of young men from Clarke County

Harriet (Phillips) – Born 1836 or1837 and died 1928 was the daughter of Juliet and spent her life with John Newton Everhart, giving birth to 9 children. She sent each of her children to a small black school in the Longmarsh District of Clarke County in order to ensure that all could read and write. Harriet did purchase 3 acres next to Jesse Russell in 1867 and in 1871 she purchased the lot in Berryville where she built a 2 story stucco house which still stands today. Her family has never forgotten her and pass on her legacy from generation to generation.

Marshall – Born 1838. Marshall was a son of Juliet and Moses and brother of Harriet's. He attempted to escape in 1853 and again at the end of the trial in 1856. He was the second slave sold at auction in 1856 just behind Juliet. Harriet named one of her sons Marshall. He was living with Harriet in the last census (1920) before her death in 1928. Marshall, the brother to Harriet, was never heard from again after the 1856 auction.

Ella Nora Phillips – Born 1893 and died 1987. Ella was the granddaughter of Harriet and attended a small rural school in Clarke County close to where her father lived called Peace and Plenty. It is believed that she later moved into Berryville where she lived with Harriet, so as to attend a black school in Berryville. She entered the all black Storer College in Harpers Ferry, Jefferson County, West Virginia when she was 12 years old and graduated at age 16. She later moved to Pittsburgh where she attended the University of Pittsburgh's School of Pharmacy where she became the first African American woman to graduate from there in 1916. She was also the first African American woman to practice in Pennsylvania. She later moved to Youngstown, Ohio with her new husband, William Wyatt Stewart, who was also a graduate of the University of Pittsburgh's School of Pharmacy. Several years later they moved to Toledo, Ohio where both continued to practice as pharmacists at her and her husband's privately owned drug store. After retiring she served in the Eisenhower administration in several different capacities. She spent 6 years with UNESCO traveling to many parts of the world as an ambassador for education. She was a life long member of the NAACP and the first president of the National Women of Colored People. Of all the honors bestowed on Ella Phillips Stewart, the one honor she most prized was a girls school named in her honor in Toledo, OH. In 1957, the Virginia Chamber of

Commerce sent her an invitation honoring "distinguished Virginians" at a dinner to recognize the 350th anniversary of Jamestown. When the Chamber discovered that she was "a negro", the invitation was rescinded.

Moses – Born 1820. Moses was likely the husband of Juliet and father of their children, but there is no documented proof to back this claim. After the slave auction in 1856, Moses was never heard from again.

Juliet (Julia) – Born 1815. Juliet was a slave of John Russell Crafton. In the will he wrote in 1839 he provided for the freedom of Juliet and all her family. By 1856, there were 14 slaves that were supposed to have been freed, but John Russell Crafton's son Bennett Russell and his siblings had Crafton sign an addendum to the original will in 1842, known as the Articles of Agreement that revoked the slave's freedom. The Articles were signed only by family members as mentioned in the story and by the mysterious William R. Spurr. The Articles failed to revoke all wills and or codicils that may have come before it. It was also obvious that an attorney had not written the Articles. Although it cannot be proven, it is highly suspected that Crafton had suffered a stroke. There is proof that he could write his name, but the Articles were supposedly signed by him with a crude "X". There was certainly reason to have had his slaves hired out to help offset any costs of his care but there was no reason why he would have made the incredible decision to sell the slaves upon his death. These factors within the Articles were pointed out by an expert in manumission wills and trials during this period of time and it was her opinion that having seen similar, the Articles had the scent of fraud about them.

Juliet and all the other slaves were actual persons involved in the will and the law suit. The law suit was called *Bennett Russell and Others vs. Negroes Juliet and Others*. It lasted 8 years from

1848 to 1856. The Articles of Agreement did exist and did revoke the slaves freedom and *was* a highly suspect document.

Juliet was transported to the courthouse in Winchester, Virginia by Thomas Gold. She was also never allowed to testify. She was the first slave to be put up on the auction block. Marshall was the second to be sold.

Juliet was never heard from again.

The author still lives in Clarke County, Virginia. The farm known as Rock Hall belonging to his 2nd great grandfather, Bennett Russell, went out of the family hands in 1956.

Race relations and opportunities for the African American has improved from days past, but the journey is far from over. Racism continues to exist and even has grown over the past 20 years, threatening all the work of those who dedicated their lives to making a world that no longer saw color, but saw instead, the person. Rev. Martin Luther King had climbed the mountain and seen the glory but for many, the glory can still only still be seen and not fully embraced. The wisdom and efforts of this man and others who dedicated their lives to equality for all, will never be forgotten. The need for more of these incredible men today is much needed in order to finish the journey.